BONSAI
Your Guide to Creating
STANDS and BENCHES

By
George Buehler

Published by:
Haskill Creek Publishing
A Division of Stone Lantern Publishing
Passumpsic, Vermont 05861, USA

BONSAI *Your Guide to Creating* STANDS and BENCHES

Copyright©2009 George Buehler
Prospect, Kentucky USA

Executive Editor: Jerry Meislik
Book design: Dennis Howke

World rights reserved. The reproduction by any means, or any use without the express written permission of the author is prohibited.

Disclaimer

Although the author and publisher have made every effort to ensure the accuracy and completeness of this book, we assume no responsibility for any errors, inaccuracies, omissions, or inconsistencies. We have acknowledged those who assisted in this book and apologize to any person or institution that may have been inadvertently omitted.

ISBN 978-1-60530-993-4

Printed in China

First Printing – September 2009

BONSAI *Your Guide to Creating* STANDS and BENCHES

Contents

Acknowledgements **5**
Chapter 1   **Introduction** **7**
Chapter 2   **Display Stand or Display Bench** **11**
Chapter 3   **Choosing the Right Spot** **14**
Chapter 4   **Designing the Area** **17**
Chapter 5   **Materials of Construction** **25**
Chapter 6   **Design and Construction** **33**
    Plan 1 – *Wood Stand* 37
    Plan 2 – *Closed-Top Wood Stand* 39
    Plan 3 – *Rotating Closed-Top Wood Stand* 42
    Plan 4 – *Locking Support Wood Stand* 43
    Plan 5 – *Concrete Block Bench* 46
    Plan 6 – *Long Concrete Block Bench* 50
    Plan 7 – *Simple Wood Top Bench* 52
    Plan 8 – *Closed Top Bench* 54
    Plan 9 – *Locking Support Bench* 56
    Plan 10 – *Shohin Bench* 58
    Plan 11 – *Stone Top Bench* 60
    Plan 12 – *Simple Shade Bench* 62
    Plan 13 – *Large Shade House Bench* 65
    Plan 14 – *Concrete Humidity Bench* 67
    Plan 15 – *Deck Corner Stand* 69
Chapter 7   **Finishing Up** **73**
Chapter 8   **Maintenance** **77**
Chapter 9   **Drawings** **81**
References **106**
Index **107**

BONSAI *Your Guide to Creating* STANDS and BENCHES

Acknowledgements

I want to thank various members of the Greater Louisville Bonsai Society for allowing me to photograph their stands and for giving me the needed information on their construction techniques. Among these are Tom McCurry, Earl Ekman, Lee Squires, Ken Popp, Richard Blaney, and John Callaway. If I have omitted anyone, my sincere apologies.

Several pictures shown here were photographed at various times when visiting bonsai hobbyists around the country. The reader will hopefully understand that some of the pictures were taken for other reasons, and may not show as completely as desired the information that is being presented.

I also want to thank various members of the American Bonsai Society for their guidance in this project, along with use of pictures and drawings of their benches and stands. What first started as a "small" guide to building stands has blossomed into this book.

Finally, I want to thank my wife for "putting up" with my passion for bonsai and always being ready to proofread my writings on the subject. Although she is not a bonsai person – whatever that means – she has the uncanny ability to read over my articles and find various flaws in the grammar, spelling, and most importantly, the context. Her diligent efforts have made my writings look more professional than they would otherwise be.

BONSAI *Your Guide to Creating* STANDS and BENCHES

Chapter 1
Introduction

We all know that bonsai are not indoor trees, and even those trees we sometimes call "indoor" trees need to be outside during the growing season. We can put our trees on a patio, deck rail, or various types of garden benches available at garden supply centers. However, after a while, we begin to realize that our prized trees would look much better if we could "exhibit" them in a more aesthetic manner. When we visit the gardens of other bonsai hobbyists and look at their trees, we often think about how beautiful their trees are. However, are we seeing the beautiful trees, what they are sitting on, the artistically designed layout, or a combination of all these?

As bonsai artists, we spend countless hours trimming, wiring, fertilizing, repotting, and watering our trees. We try to give each tree its "ideal" amount of fertilizer, water, and sunshine. Sometimes we have to move trees around to do these tasks. Because we love the hobby, we lovingly do this for one or two trees. However, these tasks become more difficult and time consuming when we have more than a few trees.

As your bonsai collection increases, you will need a place outside where they can receive the needed sunshine, where they can be displayed, and where they are safe from the outside world. This can be a display stand, a display bench, or a combination. A display stand is designed to hold one or, at most, two small bonsai. On the other hand, a display bench can hold any number of bonsai depending on the size of the bench and the size of the trees. Not only do stands and benches serve as a place to put your bonsai, but:

1. they also facilitate viewing your trees and allow for observing various problems, such as insects or disease
2. they make it easy to do some maintenance tasks such as pruning, watering, and turning your trees to expose them to sunlight from all sides
3. they allow air flow around the trees which lessens the chance of fungal disease
4. they allow trees to stand out more as focal points

The stands we will refer to herein are for outside use. When bonsai are displayed inside at exhibitions/shows, they are placed on "stands" to better show off the tree and are referred to as exhibition stands. These stands are not covered in this publication since they require extensive woodworking skills and tools. They are generally constructed out of hardwood and are of furniture quality. They can be purchased from a variety of sources in any number of styles and sizes. However, be forewarned that they can be quite expensive depending on the size, type of wood used, and style. I have seen these exhibition stands sell for as much as $1,000 from various vendors.

In chapter 5, we discuss some of the materials used for outdoor stands and benches. There are no hard and fast rules for materials used. If we list a pressure-treated wood in our material list but a non-pressure-treated wood is your preference, this is completely acceptable. The positive and negatives for the various materials which can be used are also presented in chapter 5. When we list the use of decking boards, these boards are a full 1 inch, whereas a 1 by 6 is actually ¾" thick. Therefore, some adjustments in measurements will be required if a regular 1 x 6 is used, rather than a specified decking board.

In chapter 6, there are a number of different style stands and benches listed. Depending on your particular available space and personal preferences, one design may look better than another. It may be that a combination of two suits your preferences. Or you may decide that the use of a steel post is what you want to employ rather than a wooden post. This is certainly acceptable.

Chapter 9 contains the various drawings of the stands and benches discussed in chapter 6. A number of these drawings are actual construction diagrams (i.e. drawings from which stands have been built). Others are generalized drawings which show how a particular style can be constructed. However, the generalized drawings do not have dimensions since the sizes depend on the size of wood used, and lengths can be varied to meet your particular requirements. It should be noted, that on the generalized drawings, although dimensions are not given, they were drawn to an arbitrary scale using a computer drawing program.

Although we give detailed instructions on how to construct a particular style of bonsai stand or bench, this is by no means the only way to construct it. We have tried to list several alternatives to each design. The reader should understand that the information contained here is just a guide, and many modifications can be made. Some of the factors that play a part in the design decision of stands/benches are:

- the geographic area where you live
- the climatic conditions to which the trees will be exposed
- the type of trees in the collection
- how aesthetically pleasing the stands/benches need to be

- the amount of money available for purchasing the needed materials

The choice of design and the materials chosen for building the design influence the cost. If cedar is the chosen wood for the stands, the cost will be substantially higher than if pressure-treated pine is used – at least in my area. I have also found in discussions with other bonsai hobbyists around the country that the material cost varies from state to state. There may also be the problem of availability in your particular locality. Therefore, in our discussions on materials, I have tried to list alternates that could be used. The reader should check his local lumber or big box dealers for alternatives in his area.

A person can spend a large amount of money building benches or stands. The expensive ones serve the same purpose as much simpler – and cheaper - designs. We will leave it up to you, your pocket book, and your carpentry skills to decide which designs fill your needs.

You do not need to be a skilled carpenter to make your own stands or benches. Depending on the design used, simple tools are all that may be needed to make pleasing stands or benches. In fact, some simple designs may not require any tools, only the labor needed to lay a board across an upright. Other more complicated designs require extensive woodworking skills and tools. Stands can also be purchased from several bonsai dealers if you would rather buy them. However, even if you have only rudimentary carpentry skills, I highly recommend making your own. There is a self-gratification when you put a bonsai that you have designed on a stand that you have constructed.

Some of the more popular styles of stands and benches are included in this book. However, there are more designs than could possibly be covered here. Use the pictures and drawings as a guide, but don't hesitate to modify the drawings or use the pictures interspersed throughout this book to make your own drawings. You may want to combine an aspect of one drawing with an aspect of a picture to create a stand that fits your needs. A strong recommendation before starting construction on your benches is to take a camera, ruler, and pencil and paper to gardens of other bonsai artists in your area to see (and document) what they have used. When I was going around to our club members' gardens, I often saw techniques I hadn't considered, designs that were interesting modifications, and some ingenious methods of displaying their bonsai – which, of course, is the real purpose of constructing a support.

Chapter 2
Display Stand or Display Benches

One of the first decisions to make is whether you want (or need) a display stand, a display bench, or perhaps due to the size of your collection, you need both (Picture 2-1). This will affect the size or design of the area that is needed. If there are only one or two bonsai, display stands probably are the best choice. If there are a large number of trees to accommodate, then benches, since they hold more trees, are a good choice. If there are a number of specimen trees involved, you probably wouldn't want to have them bunched together on a bench. They probably need to be on individual stands, for better visibility. It also may be that the space available is only suited for display stands. Taking extra time to decide on the current requirements, as well as doing some planning for future requirements, can save many hours of manual labor and frustration.

When I first put out one display stand, I thought that would be more than sufficient, since I had one good quality tree at the time. Therefore, I chose a spot where I could see the tree from the house and where there wasn't much competition from other garden plants. I also built several simple tables which I put by my deck. On these, I placed my 'starter' trees and some trees I purchased that still needed a lot of work. However, as my collection increased, I needed additional display area, and I couldn't put more tables on the deck. I knew I had to expand my display area. Because I think stands show off bonsai better than tables, I decided to put in additional stands next to the one I had initially installed. In retrospect, I probably should have removed the original stand, put a bench in its place and installed the stand somewhere else. The point is that before the manual labor is exerted to build and install a stand, benches should be carefully considered.

Picture 2-1

However, I didn't know at the time the basics of what was a visually pleasing area (some will say I still don't). As I had the opportunity to see other hobbyists' stands and benches and their layouts, I took pictures of what they had, observed how they had arranged their areas, and made mental notes of what I liked or disliked. I now realize that almost any arrangement of stands is acceptable. I also saw that if the area to be used for displaying bonsai was along a fence, placing a bench next to several stands could look nice. Remember, a display stand is generally meant to have one bonsai on it. Stands are more versatile in placement than benches since they are smaller. Display stands can be placed around a deck, on a fence line or almost anywhere. Since they are single units, they are more easily situated in a back yard.

As a general rule, display stands show off bonsai better than a bench. However, the drawback to stands is that they are separated from other stands. Therefore, when it comes time for watering, it will take longer to go from stand to stand than it would watering a bench full of trees. An additional drawback to stands is that, per unit area, they are generally more expensive to construct than benches.

On the positive side, because stands hold only one tree, their use allows you to more easily work on your bonsai. They also make it easier to routinely turn trees. Best of all, stands make it easier to admire your work.

Benches are basically long tables – from four feet to ten feet or longer. Because of their larger size, more thought must be given to where and how they are placed in the assigned area. They are particularly suited for placement of pre-bonsai or bonsai-in-training, or where a large number of trees need to be stored.

In areas where the temperatures and sun intensities are a concern to bonsai health, a covering to block out some of the sun during part of the day may be needed. Benches can be designed to accommodate this shade top or partial shade top to block out the sun intensity. These tops can be made of wood, or they can have a fabric covering called a shade cloth.

Later we will present several options for building both stands and benches, along with materials suitable for them and the necessary tools. We will also list where a stand can be converted into a bench and vice versa. In chapters 3 and 4 we will present how an area for benches/stands is chosen, and what to consider in choosing an area. Design precautions that are needed will also be covered.

An important consideration that must be brought into the discussion of benches and stands is the weight that the benches will hold. Certain precautions are required, to lessen the possibility of the bench uprights sinking. Since benches hold numerous bonsai pots, they may need more uprights to support the top as they get longer. They may also need a larger sized support structure, or both. There is nothing more problematic than having part of the bench sink (Picture 2-2). If an upright on a long bench did sink, the only option would be to disassemble the bench, dig out the upright, and bury another. This is not an easy task. As the bench gets longer, additional construction techniques are required to reinforce the bench. This means that the uprights may need to be sunk into the ground further, larger sized uprights used and/or the amount of lumber used for support may need to be increased. In chapter 6, we will cover some of the additional steps needed for long benches.

Picture 2-1

Also, when either benches or stands are constructed from wood, there is always the possibility of the wood warping or the uprights twisting (Picture 2-2). This is just a characteristic of some of the wood that is currently available on the market. This problem can be lessened in several ways. The bench top can be constructed from "2 by" lumber rather than "1 by" lumber. Of course, when larger lumber is used, it also requires larger screws to ensure the wood is held in place. We will deal with some of these problems in the construction chapter (Chapter 6).

Remember, many bonsai hobbyists have both bonsai stands and benches. Both can be in close proximity to each other and present a pleasing appearance. It all depends on the area chosen and how the area is laid out.

Chapter 3

Choosing the Right Spot

In choosing the right spot to place your stands or benches, there are a number of things to consider. The first thing to take into account is the location and the size of the area that can be negotiated from your spouse. Seriously, the area should meet several criteria:

1. Which area will give the best view of the tree(s) from the house or patio? Does this area have a lot of bushes that will grow and block the view of the trees? As the garden bushes grow, will they overhang the bonsai or block sunlight from the tree? Are the garden bushes a type that has showy blooms that will distract from the bonsai? Are the garden bushes in the area prone to insect or disease problems? If so, will their problems drift over to the bonsai that will be in the area? If the garden bushes need to be sprayed, are they far enough away from the bonsai area so that there will not be overspray onto the bonsai? Or, if the location is in close proximity to the garden bushes, can the insects on the bushes be hand-picked rather than controlled with insecticides? Finally on this point, if the bushes need to be sprayed and they are close to the bonsai, can the bonsai be sprayed with the insecticide at the same time as the bushes?

2. What about the safety of the area? Is it visible from the street? Unfortunately, we live in an age where we must try to protect our bonsai from unsavory characters. If this best area choice is visible from the street, can a fence or privacy bushes be installed? Does your area have deer? A marauding deer may consider a bonsai sitting out in the open on a stand to be a delectable meal. Once again, a fence may be the answer for this problem, but placing the stands/benches closer to a building may also solve this safety issue. Is the area close enough to a house or garage where motion-controlled spotlights can be installed to ward off animals of various types? Additionally, when considering safety, thought must be given to the potential for damage from footballs/basketballs thrown by neighbor children. You wouldn't want to install a row of stands adjacent to the neighbor's basketball goal.

3. Is there enough sunlight or too much? What about other 'elements', such as prevailing winds? Putting shohin bonsai on a bench that is constantly exposed to high wind is not a good idea. If the area chosen does have a

wind problem, can a screen of either plant or fence material be used to deflect it?

   4. Look at surrounding trees. Will they grow and block out the sun to the potential area, or will they be a benefit (i.e. partial shading during the day)? Also, do these trees emit anything that will get on the bonsai, (i.e. sap from a hickory or nuisance flower remnants from a mimosa)? Of course, if this is the only choice for your display area, you may have to put up with these problems.

   5. What look are you trying to achieve? Do you just want a spot to place your trees? In the future, do you want to expand your designated area into a Japanese garden?

   6. Is the area convenient for watering and other maintenance tasks? If a spot is chosen that is out of the way, chances are that insect infestation and other such problems may not be noticed until it is too late. This is especially important if an automatic watering system is employed and a daily inspection of the trees is not performed.

   7. Is the area prone to frost? If it is, you might be forced to move trees indoors and out in the early spring.

   8. Will the area look better with the benches on the perimeter of the area and stands in strategic locations on the inside? Would the reverse be more aesthetically pleasing? You might think you know what your needs are, but by all means, check with your spouse and some fellow bonsai hobbyists to get their opinion. You may not take it, but at least you may get some other ideas.

In summary, the ideal spot would be an area protected from high winds, not visible from the street, in sunlight for more than 5 to 6 hours a day and where only the pot is in the shade during the mid-afternoon. Additionally the chosen spot should be convenient for both daily watering and inspections and where the bonsai can be seen. Few bonsai enthusiasts have an area that meets all these criteria. What you need to do is to examine the area you have available and decide which location meets most of the criteria. There may be only one spot available. If this is the case, you will need to make the best of the situation and design the space the best you can.

Will the area look better with stands on one side of the property and benches on the other? If that option is not available, benches along the perimeter and stands in strategic locations is a good option.

Perhaps, as in my situation, both benches and stands had to be installed side by side in the area available. I had to decide how close to space them. There is no rule on how close stands, benches or combination of both should be. It is what appeals to you. For stands, I chose to place them a minimum of one stand length apart. I did not put two benches side by side, but I put one stand in between two benches and located them at least one stand length apart on each side.

I have listed the above criteria in what I consider to be the order of importance. However, this is based on my particular situation and area. Consideration of the wind effects may be more important than whether the stand is visible from the street, if the targeted area is constantly exposed to winds. If you live in a rural area, protection from deer and animal destruction may be more important.

Your preferences and individual factors for consideration will be unique to you. It is my hope that the guidelines presented above will help you make an informed choice.

Chapter 4
Designing the Area

We now assume that a potential spot has been chosen and we have a tentative idea of the bench/stand requirements needed. Before starting construction of the platforms, a rough sketch of the chosen area, along with existing structures, should be made so that the proposed benches/stands can be drawn in place. I use a piece of quadrille paper (paper that has ¼" or 1/8" squares printed on it). This type of paper can be obtained from an office supply store. This paper may also be used in the actual design or modifications of the benches/stands that are presented later. Designing the area can also be done on a computer if the appropriate programs are available; however, unless you are skilled in computer design, this can take more time than doing a pencil sketch. I assign a dimension to each square, such as one square equals one foot. The area is then measured and laid out on the paper. When I initially drew my chosen area, I took my pencil, paper, and tape measure outside with me and roughly laid out the area, putting in the existing trees, bushes, and house structure. I noted the time of day and how any trees shaded the area. I went back out at a later time to make sure I had the shaded areas marked. This initial sketch needs only to be a rough layout of the area, but it should be sufficiently detailed. Because my rough sketch had a lot of erasure marks on it, I redrew the whole thing, using the sketch as a guide to my dimensions (Drawing 4-1).

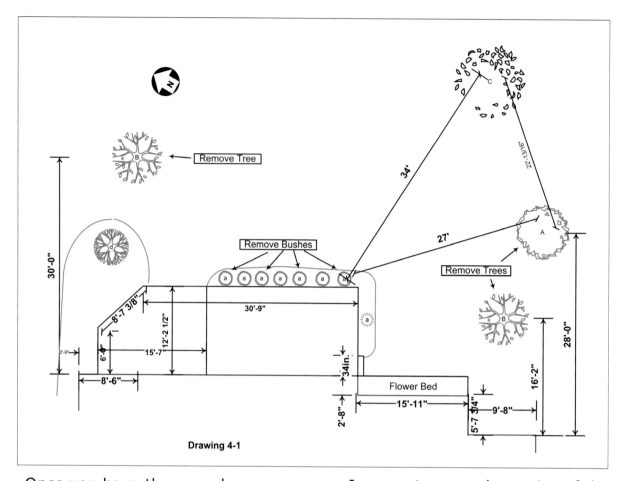

Drawing 4-1

    Once you have the area drawn on paper, I suggest you make copies of the page before drawing the proposed benches. This will save you from having to redraw the overall area again. It will also allow you to draw several proposed designs and to compare them side by side. With the area drawing in hand, go back out to the area and make sure that all bushes, structures, etc. are drawn in the appropriate spots and that the dimensions are correct. A helper is beneficial when checking the dimensions to help hold the tape measure and to look over the drawing to ensure that all the relevant structures, trees, etc. are in place. Think about what can be or should be removed and what needs to be added.

    Also make sure that any underground utilities (irrigation lines, drains, cable lines, etc.) are taken into account and are noted on the drawing. You would not want to sever a cable line or, worse, an underground electrical line when you start digging the holes for the uprights. If there are any questions about the locations of utilities, most cities offer a free service of locating and marking these utilities for you. If you have a yard irrigation system, you should consider what area the water distribution arcs cover (Drawing 4-2). If this is not considered, the display benches/stands may be flooded with water when the irrigation system comes on. Once you have a plan in mind and a rough sketch on paper, go to the chosen area and put flags in the approximate areas where you think the stands and benches will go. With the irrigation system turned on, and with the aid of a ruler to simulate the stand height, estimate how much water will hit the stand top. Mark on the drawing if the stand top will be flooded. In my design, there were a couple of tops that appeared as if they would get too much water. You may have to decide between moving the stand or having the irrigation system adjusted.

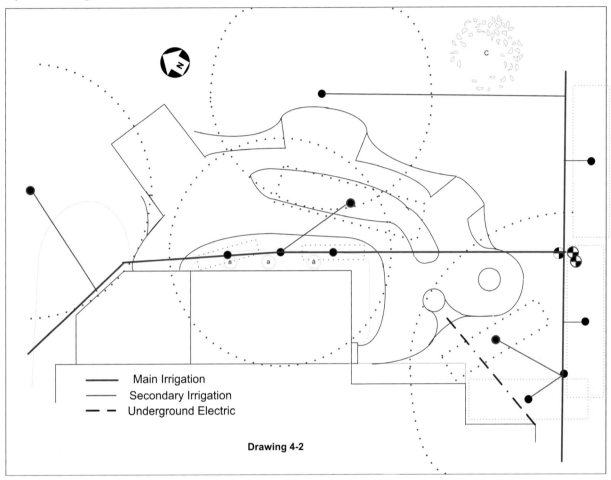

Drawing 4-2

Now, using another copy of the area, the proposed bench or stands, any pathways, and any additional shrubbery can be drawn (Drawing 4-3). As a rough approximation, each bonsai pot will need about one and a half square feet of bench space for each square foot of pot to allow for viewing and air circulation. This is only a rough approximation and will be determined by the size of the trees to be placed on the stands. If there are only shohin that need to be placed, less space will be needed than if large trees are proposed for the stands. Now is the time to plan ahead. If the collection to be displayed currently has only one or two trees, it is a good idea to design for three or four trees to allow for future collection increase, even if only one or two stands are initially constructed.

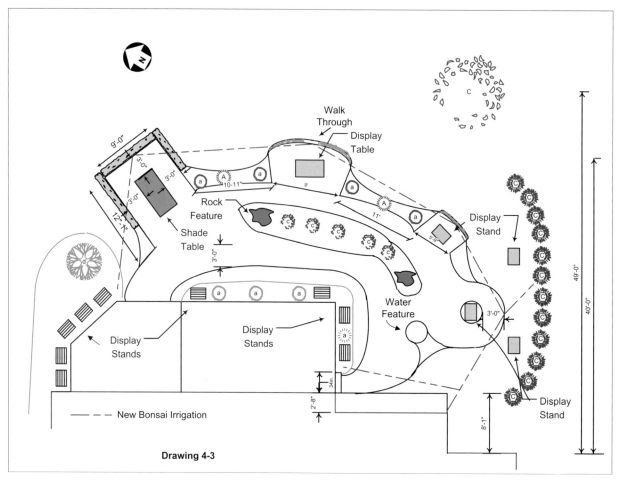

Drawing 4-3

Is the plan to put one prized specimen on a stand? What happens when another specimen tree is obtained – will it go on another stand or will it be placed on a bench? Is the area suitable for expansion or is another area better suited for expansion? These are the kinds of thoughts that must go into the design of the area for the benches/stands. I realize it is hard to predict the future; but, if you are considering building either stand or benches, I'm sure that additional trees will be added to the collection.

Another consideration is the need for a walk way to the area, if it is a distance from the house. You may decide that having a grass path is more than adequate, or a gravel path may be your choice. Either way, this needs to be built into the initial design.

Finally as the proposed area is laid out, each stand or bench should be separated from grass areas of the yard by a border. This border can be a physical border of landscape edging or it can simply be a mulched area. The mulch can be gravel or landscape mulch (such as pine bark, cypress mulch, or even pine straw). Something needs to be employed to hinder weed and grass growth around the uprights of stands and under the benches. This border should be included into the plan drawing.

How close should the stands or benches be? In chapter 3, we stated that the stand-to-stand distance should be one stand length apart. If an area is only suitable for a single line of stands, they should not be placed in a straight line; they should be offset from each other and of varying heights.

Stands are generally of a uniform size that you determine. However, you may decide that they all don't need to be of equal size. When I designed my first stand, I set the dimensions at 26" long by 18" deep. This size is more than adequate for a forest pot (approx. 20" x16"). It also worked out well for the way I constructed my stands (See Construction Chapter 6 – Plan 4). I chose to make my wood benches 18" deep to be uniform with the stands. These dimensions have worked out well for my particular layout and tree sizes. If the tree you are most interested in displaying is in a larger pot, you will have to make adjustments in the dimensions.

I have seen a number of bonsai display areas where the stands were of varying sizes. Putting a 26" x 18" stand directly next to a 36" x 24" stand is not aesthetically pleasing to me. My attention is drawn away from the bonsai to the stands, which is not the reason for building the stands. However, if a large stand is placed on opposite sides of the chosen area or if there is some sort of visual break in between, such as a bush, there is no problem. If there will be a number of stands of several sizes, I would suggest two scenarios:

1. Start at one end and increase the sizes from the smallest to the largest.
2. Place the largest stand in the center of the chosen area, and then work outward until the smallest are on the outside.

Picture 4-1

If you are going to use stone for either your stands or benches (Picture 4-1), you will need to find out what sizes are available in your area. Additionally, if stands are to be made with stone tops, the stone quarry can cut the stones to almost any size you desire. However, the more cutting that is done, the higher the price of the stone. In general, I would recommend the use of stone tops only for benches due to the high costs involved to have the stones cut and the increased difficulty attaching the stones to an upright (See chapter 6 on how this is done).

An additional point to consider while laying out the positions of the display stands is their height above ground. This point is probably the hardest on which to give good guidelines. Everything I have read regarding bonsai viewing states that they should be viewed at eye level. If the viewer is 5 foot tall, making the stand at that level may be difficult and unsightly. After looking at display heights used by other bonsai people, I constructed my stands to be approximately 3 to 4 feet above ground. However, varying the heights of stands placed side by side also makes an attractive setting (picture 4-2). There is no magic "rule" for display heights. The heights I chose were determined by:

Picture 4-2 Courtesy of Riener Goebel

- what I thought looked best in the area where the stands were placed
- how high nearby garden bushes were going to be allowed to grow
- whether there were going to be several stands in the vicinity (I didn't want them to be all the same height. Therefore, I would find the height of the primary stand, then I would lower the ones next to it to give a pleasing appearance.)
- the amount of sun or shade the bonsai would receive during the day (If, by lowering the stand several inches, the pot would be in the shade during the hottest part of the afternoon, then I lowered it. This is one of the reasons I noted the amount of shade the area received when I laid out the area. Likewise, I raised the stands on which my tropicals were to be placed, so they would receive the maximum amount of sun/heat during the hottest part of the day.)

I had the greatest difficulty in determining the "ideal" height for several of my stands that were to be placed around the perimeter of the deck. Since the deck is about one foot higher than the surrounding ground level, I had to decide whether I wanted to be able to see the tree from the deck and have it slightly high for viewing when standing on the ground outside the deck, or have it lower than the deck rail and a better height for viewing when standing on the ground. What I initially ended up doing was to make these stands level with the deck railing, so that I could see the trees from the deck. Later, I lowered a couple of these stands to break the "level" look that the stands appeared to have when they were at the same height as the deck rail. Each situation will be different than mine, so you will have to decide the best height based on your particular layout. I would suggest that, as you try to decide on the height of your stands, it is better to set them on the higher side at first. The uprights can be shortened later, but to try to raise an upright is a major undertaking.

Because benches are set up for a slightly different purpose, their height is usually easier to determine. I chose 36 to 40 inches for the height of all my benches, including what I call my shade table (this is a large bench with an overhead framework, where I can put trees that are more sensitive to the summer heat or which need less sun to prosper). For me, this is an ideal height to work on the trees and to water them.

In summary, when designing a display area, some of the points to consider are:

- how many stands and benches will be constructed in the area
- where the platforms are to be placed
- the size of both the benches and stands
- the height of each and if it will be inundated by a yard irrigation system
- if there are underground utilities to design around
- if and where there will be yard accent plants utilized

Chapter 5
Materials of Construction

There are many options when it comes to materials that can be used for your platforms. The look that is desired in the finished product and your construction skills will dictate the type of materials. We will start from the ground up and give several options as we first virtually build our displays.

Uprights

Uprights can be made from timbers, steel posts, concrete blocks, or even bricks. If timbers are used, in most cases, they should be a minimum of 4" x 4". They can be square, square with slightly rounded corners, rectangular with two rounded sides (which is termed "landscape timber"), or completely round. They can even be individual boards nailed together to form a square or a slightly fancier square (drawing 5-1 Chapter 9). I use square posts since the square sides make it easier to attach the supports for the top. However, if you prefer the look that the round landscape timbers give, it is only slightly more difficult to attach the tops. Pressure-treated wood should be used since the uprights need to be buried in the ground and will be exposed to daily water. This type of wood will last for a minimum of 15 years buried in the ground. For larger benches, 6" x 6" timbers can also be used, but they look rather 'clunky' if they are of any significant height above ground. On the other hand, the 6" x 6" posts can look rather attractive when used for short stands to display a forest. Cedar posts can also be used if they are available in your area, but they will probably be more expensive. Cedar will last 15 to 20 years. If the decision is made to make the uprights out of individual boards (as in drawing 5-1), they can be made out of cedar, pressure-treated deck boards, or regular '"1 by"' wood, sealed with an exterior wood sealer.

No matter what type of wood is used for the upright, each piece of wood should be inspected carefully at the time of purchase. It is most important to verify that the upright is not bowed or twisted. Also, examine it for the size of any knots, and their location. If there are small knots, this is generally not a problem. If the knots are large (greater than 1"), they are almost certainly going to give you trouble in the future by twisting or bowing at the location of the knot. If the knot is within a foot of the end of the post and the full length of the post is going to be used, put that piece back and select another because that one will give you twisting and bending around the knot as the post dries. If only a portion of the post is going to be used and the section with the knot can be cut off, it should be fine to purchase.

Round steel posts can also be used for uprights. The disadvantage of steel posts is that they are prone to rusting which will cause subsequent weakening, and require periodic painting to maintain a finished look. Attaching a wooden top to a steel post is slightly more difficult than attaching it to a wood upright. Although steel posts can be used, steel posts are usually not the best choice. The life expectancy of a steel post is highly dependent on the level of maintenance provided.

Although covered more thoroughly in the section on construction, it should be noted that the steel or wood uprights should be buried a minimum of 30-36 inches in the ground to provide stability for either benches or stands. Unless you live in a very cold region, this will also be below the frost line, which is the distance below ground level that will not freeze during "normal" winters. Posts that are not buried below the frost line are likely to become dislodged by heaving from the freeze-thaw cycle. Soft soil (i.e. sandy) may require deeper or larger holes with concrete to stabilize the uprights.

Picture 5-1 Courtesy of Reiner Goebel

Concrete blocks or bricks can also be successfully used for supports, especially if a bench is being built. However, they should be placed on a concrete pad to provide stability. Additionally, concrete blocks (and especially bricks) normally require a mortared construction (i.e. use of mortar to secure the blocks/bricks together, as in a brick house). This requires a skill level beyond most of us. Concrete blocks can be used without mortar if concrete is used to fill the hollow portion of each block (see construction of concrete block benches for more details). The initial cost for blocks is higher than timber, but, if laid properly, they should last forever. However, remember that if this construction technique is used, they are almost impossible to move. If you wish to avoid this constraint, concrete blocks can be used for a temporary upright by simply placing them on a concrete patio.

I have also seen uprights made out of concrete. In this instance the top was made out of thick granite. Concrete uprights can be square, round, or almost any shape. They can also include decorative designs. If concrete uprights are made, they should be reinforced with steel rebar in order to make them more permanent and more resistant to the effects of freezing. This type of upright will not be covered since this is beyond the ability of most of our skillsets.

Finally, flue tile can be used to make short display stands (see Picture 5-1) or to act as uprights for short benches. Flue tiles are used on the inside of chimneys to allow the smoke to exit from fireplaces or gas burning furnaces and water heaters. They typically come in two foot sections, although longer lengths (3 or 4 feet) can be found. For some applications, they can be used to make attractive short stands.

Tops

Both stands and benches can be made from pressure-treated decking boards (1" x 6" boards), pressure-treated 'two by' boards, pine boards (sealed later), redwood, cedar, or almost any available wood. Use of redwood or cedar will increase the cost substantially while not necessarily providing longer life than pressure-treated wood. Stone or, for that matter, concrete can also be used for tops. Wood is the generally preferred choice for tops since it is easy to work with and a number of different styles can be made. The tops can be a single piece of wood or they can be made of pieces spaced sufficiently apart to allow for water run-off. Depending on the thickness of the wood and the way the tops are constructed, they can be capable of holding very heavy loads.

I have seen man-made boards constructed out of wood chips, saw dust, or ground up plastic that are sold as replacements for natural boards in deck building. I have not tried this type of material, but based on the cost of the boards, I find it hard to justify its use. In addition, although touted to have a substantially longer life with no warping, twisting or splintering, they are relatively new and do not have a lengthy track record.

Picture 5-2

While discussing wood used in stands or benches, I need to mention wood sizes. All wood is listed in even inch sizes, such as 1 x 4, 2 x 4, 4 x 4, etc. Actually a 1 x 4 is ¾" x 3½", a 2 x 4 is 1½" x 3 ½", a 4 x 4 is 3½" x 3 ½". A standard deck board is 1 1/8" x 5 ½". These dimensions are important if, when using a drawing presented in chapter 9, a different size board is substituted or if a plan is modified.

Although stone can be used for stand tops, it is normally only used for display benches. Picture 5-2 shows a bench top constructed from granite. A top of this size would be very expensive, but it offers a distinct look. Sandstone is a common material in my area that can be used for stone tops. It is readily available from stone suppliers, is relatively cheap compared to granite, and can be purchased smooth and polished. A slab of sandstone approximately 1 to 2 inches thick is normal. A slab of sandstone that is 2 inches thick and measures 24 inches by 48 inches will weigh several hundred pounds. Granite of the same dimensions would be approximately twice this weight. The major disadvantage to stone tops, other than the weight (and potential cost), is that they are slippery when wet. Bonsai could actually slide off of them in a driving rain. In addition, care needs to be practiced when working around the stone top benches to ensure that the stone doesn't get chipped or cracked. Attachment to the upright also requires different techniques which are discussed in chapter 6.

Picture 5-3

If the bonsai artist is ambitious, a concrete top can be made that acts as a humidity tray (Picture 5-3), or it can be made flat. Both will require building a form to hold the wet concrete that you either hand mix or purchase pre-mixed. If either type top is of any size, it will require a number of people to move. The concrete humidity trays also require periodic cleaning to remove collected debris and algae.

Method of Attachment

When wood is used for both the top and uprights, the tops will need to be secured to the uprights. This can be done with nails, screws, or bolts. Screws are the preferred choice since they hold the various members together better than nails and are less likely to work loose. Bolts are generally only used for large benches or when attaching a wood top to a steel post. Screws should either be coated deck screws or, preferably, stainless steel. Ordinary steel screws or nails will quickly rust out and lose their holding power. I have had steel screws rust through within one growing season. The stainless screws are about 1.5 times the cost of deck screws and about two times the cost of steel screws. I have not had a support failure since I started using the stainless. I use a 305 stainless screw called either a Robertson® screw or, by some suppliers, a square drive screw. This type of screw has a square recess in the head to drive it in. Substantially more force can be used with this type of screw head than with a regular slotted or Phillips head screw, and there is little chance of stripping the head, which can occur with these other choices.

No matter what screw type is used, a pilot hole should be drilled to avoid the possibility of breaking the screw or splitting the wood. When drilling the pilot hole, the hole should go through the first mating piece and into the second piece almost as deep as the screw will penetrate. The normal practice when evaluating the length of the screw is to try to have about ½ to 2/3 of the screw length threaded into the secondary piece. If two 2 x 4 boards are to be connected to form an 'L', a screw 3" to 4" long would be used. Typically, when using 'one by' wood, a number 6 or 8 screw size is used. For 'two by' material, a number 8 or 10 is normal. If there will be a number of heavy bonsai supported by a bench, you might consider using a number 12 screw. The larger the screw, the more holding power it will have. When securing the end of a board, keep in mind that the larger the screw, the further the screw should be from the edge of the board to avoid splitting it – even with a pilot hole. Using our example above of securing two 2 x 4 boards, the screw should be centered on the inner board (Picture 5-4).

Picture 5-4

One final word on the length and size of screws. If in joining two boards, the screw will be driven into the wood with the grain of the wood (as are the two screws on the left side of picture 5-4), they should be longer than screws being driven across the grain (screws on the right side of picture 5-4). This is because when driving screws with the grain, the wood fibers are basically only being pushed aside. However when driving a screw across the grain, the wood fibers are actually being severed. The screws on the left of picture 5-4 are #8 4-inch screws. The ones on the right are #8 3-inch screws. Alternately, screws being driven into the grain could be a larger size, i.e. the screws on the left could have been #10 3-inch screws.

If the uprights used are steel posts and the tops are wood, the tops are secured to the posts with bolts. When the tops are stone, a number of methods can be used and are described in Chapter 6 on construction.

When blocks or flue tiles are used for uprights, the tops are laid across the blocks or tiles, with no attaching screws or bolts.

Dry Mix Concrete

This material is often called Quikrete® or Sakrete® and is purchased from building supply centers. It is used to stabilize uprights in the ground. It comes in 40 to 80 pound bags, depending on the brand, and a 60 pound bag typically costs $4 to $6. When using a post hole digger to dig the holes for the uprights, one 60 pound bag will secure about 4 to 5 uprights. This same material is used to make concrete pads for supporting blocks, brick, or flue tiles. When handling this material, gloves should be worn since it is somewhat caustic to the skin. Also, a dust mask should be worn when handling the mix to prevent breathing the dust.

Wood Sealer

Whether pressure-treated or non-pressure-treated wood is used, the wood will need 'sealing' to protect it from the daily exposure of water. Once the bench or stand is positioned, it should be treated with the wood sealer. Since I almost always use pressure-treated wood and I always let the pieces dry for a week or so before I start using them, I normally wait about a week after construction before sealing the wood. I have found that after this period of time, the wood is dry enough to apply the sealer. Most pressure-treated wood manufacturers recommend waiting 30 to 60 days before applying the sealer. This recommendation is made for pressure-treated wood that is used on a deck which is exposed to water from intermittent rain. Since bonsai stands receive daily watering, I prefer to apply the sealer as soon as possible to give them as much protection as possible.

There are a number of wood sealer brands on the market, and no brand recommendation can be made. You can check with neighbors to see which brand they use and how well it holds up. If someone tells you that they have to reseal their deck every other year, then you should probably stay away from that brand, since the useful life will be much shorter on a bonsai stand.

I use a brand of sealer on my stands that lasts two seasons. The same sealer lasted almost four years on my deck. I do not strip the old sealer before putting on a new coat. I wash the stands with a bleach solution, flush them well with plain water, then scrub the stand with a soap solution, followed by another water flush. After a wait of two or three days, I apply the new coat of sealer. When the wood is freshly sealed, water will bead up on the surface of the wood. You will know when the wood needs to be resealed when the water no longer beads and appears to penetrate into the wood. There is more information about sealing in Chapter 8, Maintenance.

Construction Glue

Construction glue can be used to secure stone tops to uprights of wood or steel. It comes in containers called caulking tubes. It is fairly impervious to weather and makes a strong bond between metal and stone or stone and wood. When handling this glue, gloves should be worn since it can cause a rash in some people. Its use is discussed in Chapter 6, in the stone top bench construction section.

Chapter 6
Design and Construction

There are more designs for benches and stands than we can possibly cover in this book. I have picked several different types to highlight differences. One could combine portions of two or more designs that follow into one unit that meets a particular requirement. When dimensions are given, it should be noted that these are only guidelines based on what I have constructed or what I have seen used by other bonsai hobbyists. There is no rule that says a bench has to be a certain size. It should be sized to meet one's unique space or bonsai requirements.

In the discussions of the various benches/stands that follow, I have gone into detail about the actual construction of a particular type of bench or stand when a new building technique is introduced. As we progress to different types, I only provide details for new techniques that are required to complete that project. Therefore, if the reader has questions about a construction technique that is not described in that plan, refer back to previous plans. The method listed for constructing a project is in no way the only method to use. Any number of procedures can be implemented to accomplish the project; therefore, use the methods listed as a guide and modify them to suit your situation. Likewise, in the list of materials, some actual lumber amounts are given to make a specific stand. In others, only a generalized list of materials is given – generally for benches – since the finished dimensions of the bench can be almost any size.

Before starting construction, all wood materials needed for the platforms should be purchased, tools should be gathered, and a helper should be procured (especially if large benches or stone top benches are being built). If the stands/benches are to be made from pressure-treated wood, I recommend that the materials be purchased at least a week or two prior to beginning construction. Place the wood in a single layer on a pair of saw horses in a protected area, such as a garage or dry basement, to allow it to dry. I use a basement equipped with a dehumidifier for this drying period. Most treated wood, when initially purchased, is wet with the preservative. Working with it at this stage is messy and not very healthy. It is always surprising to me how fast the wet wood seems to dry in a dehumidified basement. If KDAT (kiln dried after treatment) wood (a more expensive option), is used, construction can begin immediately. Likewise, construction can begin at any time if cedar or any untreated wood is your wood of choice.

Over the last few years, I have noticed that pressure-treated wood boards, and also regular untreated pine boards have a tendency to warp quickly. This is probably due to there being a higher moisture content in the wood now than in the past. Trying to work with a warped board is, at best, difficult and can be dangerous, especially when trying to cut it. Once a board is warped, it is almost impossible to get good results. Unless you are a very experienced woodworker, it is probably better to discard that board and replace it with a straight one.

When constructing a wood stand or bench, the end of the boards used for the top should be examined to find their growth rings. When using the boards, the growth ring should face downward (see picture 6-1). The boards have a natural tendency to 'cup' (bow in the direction of the growth rings). If they are installed with the growth rings up, they will cup quickly as they are exposed to

Picture 6-1

the daily wetting and drying. Cupping will result in an uneven surface that leads to unsightly benches or stands. When boards are installed with the growth ring down, they seldom cup.

Tools

Any of the tools listed below may be needed to construct a specific design. This is in no way a recommendation to go out and buy all of them before you start construction. There are a number of ways to complete the stands highlighted below. However, before you start, look over the tool recommendation for building each design. There I will list the tools I consider necessary. This is a list of tools that I think will make it easier to build that particular design. However, remember that when I list a power tool like a power saw, a hand saw will also do the job but will require more time and effort. You should also contact your fellow bonsai friends to determine if they could lend you one of the needed tools.

- **Post hole digger** – It can be obtained from hardware stores or home improvement centers and costs about $20. It can also be rented from a home improvement center or hardware store. It is used for digging the hole to set the uprights in. I strongly recommend using one of these for the upright hole since a nice uniform hole will be obtained. With a post hole digger, a 36 inch deep hole can be dug in a relatively short period of time, but it does require a lot of manual labor. If you are going to erect a number of stands or benches at one time, a power post hole digger can be rented from some home improvement centers. These power diggers make digging the holes faster, but their use may require the assistance of a helper since they are heavy and somewhat unwieldy.

- **Shovel** – Depending on the type of structure being built, a shovel will be needed for moving soil. A long handled digging shovel will save a lot a back strain and eliminate some of the need to bend over. A spade may also be used for some digging chores.

- **Saw** – Although most of the stands/benches can be constructed with a hand saw, it will require a lot of effort. The use of a portable power saw or a table saw will make the job much easier and result in a much neater job. Some of the designs presented later will definitely require the use of a table saw, and these will be noted. If you are not familiar with the use of these power saws, see if you can get the help of another bonsai enthusiast who has experience using them to do the required sawing. Some lumber dealers or home centers will cut the wood for you at a price, but you should consider this only if you can not find a friend to help you. If you plan on purchasing a power saw or table saw for this and other jobs, remember that this type of tool can be extremely dangerous if not used properly.

- **Wood level or laser level** – Either of these tools are necessary if benches are being constructed to ensure that the top of the uprights are level and the uprights are perpendicular to the ground. The level can be either 24" or 48". The 24" type is easier to handle. But the 48" gives better accuracy over longer distances. Laser levels are very accurate; however, they are difficult to use in the outdoors unless they are of the high end construction type (**read expensive!**). If one of the cheaper "picture hanging" types is chosen, it can be used outdoors but only on a cloudy day or in a shaded area. Laser levels can also be rented if desired.

- Miscellaneous tools:
- hammer
- screwdriver (18 volt battery operated drill is best if available – it will save a lot of time)
- 6' folding ruler used for measuring during construction
- steel tape measure (15 or 25') for laying out area and other measuring

- a framing square or carpenters square (preferred)
- caulking gun (used for application of construction cement for attaching the stone tops)
- wood scraps for supporting uprights while setting them in permanent position
- wood clamps which may be needed during the erection of the stands. Inexpensive clamps can be found at the big box stores and some hardware stores.

Helpers

It is a good idea to have one or more "willing" helpers around when starting construction or assembly since they increase the speed of completion of the project and lessen a lot of the frustrations. When enlisting the aid of helpers, make sure they can reschedule for another time if there needs to be a 'rain date'.

Designs

I will now present various designs that can be used for either stands or benches. Where possible, I will show a picture of the actual stand or bench, present a dimensional drawing (where needed), and give a list of the specific materials needed to construct it. Of course, if you decided to alter the dimensions, the list of material will be different. I also assume that an area has been chosen and checked for any underground utilities, and all preliminary site work has been accomplished (i.e. removal of existing plants, grass, etc.). A basic knowledge of construction techniques is also assumed. If you do not possess this knowledge, try to find a woodworker who can assist you in the construction.

Plan 1 - *Wood Stand*

Wood stands can range from very simple designs to the very complex ones. The upright can be wood or metal, depending on the look that is desired. As discussed earlier, a flue tile could be placed on a patio or concrete stepping stone and a single board laid across it to form a wood stand. Picture 6-2 shows what an imaginative artist did when a large American holly tree died. We will start with a simple all wood stand and then progress with more complex variations.

Picture 6-2

Bill of Materials
- 1 – 8' long 4 x 4 pressure-treated upright or 8' round post
- 1 – 4' long 2" x 12" pressure-treated board
- 1 – 4' long 2" x 4" pressure-treated board
- 5 – 4 ½" #10 stainless steel screws
- 4 – 3" #8 stainless steel screws
- 1 – 40 lb bag Quikrete®

Must-Have-Tools
- Post hole digger
- Hammer
- Saw
- Screwdriver
- Level
- Wood clamps (not essential but will make the plumbing of the upright easier)

Picture 6-3

Construction

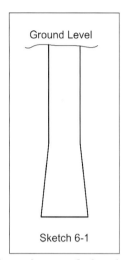
Sketch 6-1

Dig a hole approximately 30" to 36" deep with the post hole digger. This is a standard depth, at least in my area, that is below the frost line. Also at this depth, there is little chance of the uprights working loose from other forces. When digging the hole, try to keep it fairly uniform all the way to the bottom. To add stability to the upright, widen the bottom of the hole, once the proper depth is obtained (Sketch 6-1). Slide the upright into the hole and plumb the upright. Plumb means to ensure the post is exactly vertical on all sides. Using a few extra pieces of boards, prop the upright so that it doesn't move. This can be accomplished by either tacking the board to the upright or using a clamp to hold the board to the upright. The support boards should be clear of the hole. Pour some of the dry concrete mix into the hole and, using a thin board, push it down the hole to ensure there is no gap in the dry mix. This is done to make sure the mix doesn't have voids, not to compact it. Try to avoid knocking any dirt down the hole while the dry mix is being added. Dirt inadvertently being knocked into the hole is not a major problem, but a stronger support will be obtained if no dirt is included in the cement. Continue adding the dry mix into the hole while ensuring there are no gaps and that the upright is still plumb. Once the hole is completely filled, spray the top of the dry mix with just enough water to turn the dry mix a dark gray. Allow the post to set overnight or, preferably, for several days in order for the dry mix to adsorb water from the ground and harden. Leave the extra pieces of attached boards holding the upright level for several days while the cement mix is hardening. Once the cement is hard, the boards used to support the upright can be easily removed.

Cut a piece from the 2 x 12 about 16" long. Center the board from end to end and side to side on top of the upright. Drill one pilot hole in the center of the board and secure it to the upright with the 4 ½" screw. Then add two additional #10 screws to secure the top to the upright.

Cut two 6" pieces from the 2 x 4 and secure each one to the upright– on opposite sides – using two 3" screws on each board. Make sure that each of the short pieces is pushed up tight against the 2 x 12 top before securing them. Drive one 4 ½" screw from the top into each of the 2 x 4 support boards (Picture 6-3).

Construction Hints
- Although adding the dry mix cement to the hole is recommended, it is not necessarily required, depending on the soil type in your chosen area. If the soil is a clay type, the dirt removed to create the hole can

be placed back in the hole, a little at a time, and then it is compacted using a sufficiently long piece of wood. Compacting is accomplished by placing the long board into the hole and hitting the top of the piece with a hammer, settling the soil. Work around all sides of the upright. If this method is employed, the dirt should be relatively dry. As it is dug out, it should be placed on a solid surface or in a wheel barrow so that it can be broken up with a shovel prior to placing it back into the hole. The key to this method is to make sure the dirt that is added back completely fills the void around the upright and is firmly compacted in the hole. When I use this method, I usually add a small amount of the soil back into the hole at a time, compacting it as I go. When the hole is filled to about one half the distance to the top, I add some water to the hole and let the water help settle the dirt. (Note: add the water slowly, a little at a time, and wait for it to seep down. Then add some more. Stop adding the water when it takes about a minute to seep down.) I wait a day for the water to somewhat dry up then finish filling the hole with dirt that I continue to compact.

- When the compacted dirt back-fill method is used, there is no need to expand the bottom of the hole. This is only necessary when cement is used to fill up the hole.

- I usually add a half brick to the bottom of the hole prior to setting the upright into it. This helps distribute the weight of the stand and lessens the possibility of the bottom of the wood post acting as a water wick. Roofing tar or a similar sealer can be painted into the grain on the end of the wood post that goes into the hole. This seals the pores in the wood post, which also helps prevent any water wicking into the post. Water wicking into the wood will encourage rotting.

- I put the full 8' post into the ground and set it as described above before I cut the post to the desired height. Once the post is set, either using the dry mix concrete or the compacted soil technique, I measure the desired height above ground and cut the post. This ensures that the planned height is still achieved in case the hole dug is either too deep or too shallow.

Plan 2 – *Closed-Top Wood Stand*

Since the simple stand top above is not very wide (11¼"), we can increase the depth and length by using a different design (drawing 6-1). This top was made from regular wood (not pressure-treated) and will have to be sealed prior to use. Also note that the tools needed are the same as the simple top design above.

Bill of Materials
- 1 – 8' long 4 x 4 pressure-treated upright
- 2 – 8' long 1 x 4 boards
- 1 – 8' long 2 x 2 board
- 8 – 2" #8 stainless steel screws (or 4 – 2" and 4 – 3" see construction details)
- 16 – 1 1/2" #8 stainless steel screws
- 4 – 3" #8 stainless steel screws
- 1 – 40 lb bag Quikrete®

Construction

Set an upright into the ground and secure it with the dry concrete mix or the compacted soil method. Then cut the upright to the desired height as described above.

Construction of this top starts with building the outside 1 x 4 frame. Cut the frame pieces to the dimensions shown in the drawing, or alternatively, to the dimensions you need (Drawing 6-1). Using the 2" screws, secure the pieces together. Once the frame is put together, measure down ¾" on the side pieces (short pieces) and with the square, draw a line on each piece. Measure the distance front to back on the inside of the end pieces and, using these dimensions, cut two pieces from the 2 x 2 board. Put the pieces into the frame and adjust the pieces until their tops are on the line previously drawn. Secure them to the end pieces using the 2" screws. Measure the distance side to side for the top pieces and cut 4 pieces from the 1 x 4 board. Place these pieces into the frame on top of the side supports and drive 2 of the 1 1/2" screws into each piece, securing it to the side supports. Make sure there is a gap (approx ¼") between the boards so that water can drain through.

The hard part now is putting the horizontal supports in. There are three ways to do this.

The first is to measure the distance side to side between the two side supports and cut two pieces this length from the 2 x 2. With the square, mark a line on the inside of each piece 8¼" from each end of the boards. This assumes you are using the dimensions given in drawing 6-1. Line up the marks with a side of the upright and clamp both support pieces to the 4x4 upright (previously set in place), making sure the tops of the supports are in line with the top of the upright. Carefully place the top on the upright and supports and center it up, front to back, with the upright. Once you are sure the top is centered, secure the horizontal supports to the 4 x 4 with one 3" screw on each side. Remove the clamps and clamp the top assembly to the supports. The top can now be secured to the horizontal 2 x 2 supports using the 1 1/2" screws. Drive one more 3" screw on each side of the 2 x 2 horizontal supports.

The second method is to lay the top assembly on its back, center the horizontal supports on it leaving a 3 ½" space between them for the upright. Make sure the 4 x 4 upright is actually 3 ½". I have had pieces that measured 3 3/8" to 3 5/8". Clamp the 2 x 2 pieces to the top, turn it over and secure the top to the horizontal supports using the 1 1/2" screws. Then put the top on the upright and screw it to the upright.

In the third method all the 2x2 supports are assembled together prior to attaching the side 2 x 2 support pieces to the 1 x 4 outside frame. Using a scrap piece of the 4 x 4, stand it on end on a flat surface. Lay the horizontal 2 x 2 supports on the flat surface and clamp them to the 4 x 4. The side supports 2 x 2's are attached to the horizontal supports with the 3" screws. Then this assembly is slipped into the outside frame and secured.

Construction Hints

- When the top frame is being put together, use one screw in each piece while each side is being attached. This way, it is slightly easier to make sure the frame is square prior to putting the second screw into each piece. After it is checked for square, an additional screw can be driven.

- The top pieces can be rotated 90 degrees so that, rather than the top pieces being oriented side to side, they would run front to back. This would require putting the 2 x 2 support pieces on the front and back rather than on the side. The horizontal supports used to attach the top to the upright can be secured to the outside frame using screws driven from the outside of the frame pieces. Note: all four 2 x 2 support pieces would then run in the same direction – side to side.

- An interesting modification to this design can be incorporated by having a lip on the top of this design – useful for keeping shohin or small bonsai from being blown off a stand. Rather than putting the supports ¾" below the top of the frame, they can be lowered to 1" to 1 ½" and the top boards laid onto them. This will then result in a stand with an outside lip. Drawing 6-2 shows the design with the supports lowered to 1 ¼", which results in a ½" lip. A larger lip can be obtained by substituting a 1 x 6 for the 1 x 4 outer boards. The support boards can be lowered an appropriate distance to give up to a 3" lip.

Plan 3 – *Rotating Closed-Top Wood Stand*

One of the bonsai maintenance tasks that we must perform on a regular basis is to rotate the bonsai so they receive sunlight on all sides. The simple wood stand presented in Plan 1 or the closed top wood stand (Plan 2) can be modified so that the stand top can be rotated. To accomplish this, a "lazy Susan" mechanism is employed. This can be purchased at the big box stores or ordered online. The mechanism comes in several types. Do not get the type for a television unless the bonsai to be set on the stand is very heavy. This type is designed to hold a television of 200+ pounds and is extremely hard to turn.

In Plan 1, rather than screw the 2 x 12 directly to the upright post, a 1 x 10 or another 2 x 12 is first secured to the upright with 3" #10 screws. The "lazy Susan" mechanism is then secured to this 1 x 10 or 2 x 12. The top 2 x 12 is then attached to the "lazy Susan" mechanism (See Construction Hints).

For Plan 2, a few more details need to be addressed. Since the closed-top wood stand has the outside skirt, neither a rectangular or square support can be used to hold the rotating mechanism. Otherwise, when the top is rotated it will hit the sides of the skirt. The only way this can be overcome is to either use a round support plate or to shorten the skirt. After looking at several prototypes, I have found the most secure method is to attach a 1 x 12 or 1 x 10 to the bottom of the horizontal supports (the size of this board depends on the size of the rotating mechanism used). This will bring the bottom of the "1 by" material almost below the bottom of the skirt. With the lazy Susan mechanism attached, the stand top can move freely (Drawing 6-3).

Construction Hints

- For Plan 1, the mechanism has to be secured to both the top and bottom support boards. There is an access hole in both the top and bottom of the mechanism to allow attaching the screws. First center the mechanism on each board and mark where it should be attached. Then mark where the access hole is on the bottom board. Drill a hole of the appropriate size in the bottom board, attach the bottom board to the upright and then attach the mechanism to the bottom board. Lay the top board on this assembly at the proper location and, using the access hole previously drilled in the bottom board, attach the mechanism to the top board.
- For Plan 2, a similar procedure can be used.

- In order to keep the mechanism from freely rotating, a stop has to be used. A wedge can be inserted between the bottom and top "lazy Susan" attachment boards to prevent any movement.

Plan 4 – *Locking Support Wood Stand*

This top is slightly different and requires slightly more carpentry skills. In addition you will need a table saw to cut the supports. If this is the design you prefer and there is no table saw available, check with one of your local bonsai club members to determine if someone can cut the wood for you. You may also check with one of the home improvement stores or look for a local woodworking club. You're sure to find someone there to cut the wood needed for this plan, and I'm sure they will do it for a reasonable price.

Bill of Materials
- 1 – 8' long 4 x 4 pressure-treated upright
- 1 – 12' long pressure-treated decking board (1 x 6) or 1-8' long 1 x 6 pressure-treated decking board (See construction Hints below)
- 1 – 8' long 2 x 4 pressure-treated board
- 1 – 4' long 2 x 2 pressure-treated board
- 44 – 2" #8 stainless steel screws
- 8 – 2 ½" 8 stainless steel screws
- 4 – 3" #8 stainless steel screws
- 1 – 40 lb bag Quikrete®

Construction
Set an upright into the ground and secure it with the dry concrete mix or the compacted soil method. Then cut it to the desired height as previously described.

Construction of this stand starts by cutting the 12' pressure-treated 1 x 6 decking board into five 26" pieces. Then each of these boards is cut to

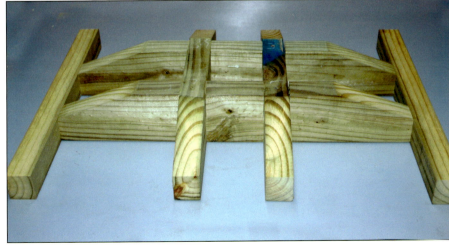

Picture 6-4

a width of 3 3/8" (See Construction Hints). The cut sides are treated with sealer and allowed to dry. While waiting for the sealer to dry, the under supports are cut to size, the finger joints cut, and the angles cut. Note that the longest board has the open part of the finger joint facing down to help prevent water getting into the joint. The four boards are then slipped together (drawings 6-4 to 6-6 and Picture 6-4). Once they are together and verified to be square, a 2 ½" #8 screw is driven into each finger joint to secure the pieces together. The end pieces are then fastened with the remaining 2 ½" #8 screws. Lay the cut decking boards on a flat surface and clamp them together with ¼" spacers in between each board (use a piece of ¼" plywood to get the proper spacing between each board). The top assembly (Picture 6-5) is then laid on top of the support structure and, after measuring the proper overhang (approximately ½"), it is secured to the support structure with 2" #8 screws. The stand top can then be put onto a 4" x 4" post and fastened to the post using the 3" #8 screws.

Picture 6-5

Construction Hints

- The 1 x 6 eight foot board can be used as is, rather than being cut into the 3 3/8" pieces. Using three 26" pieces of the 1 x 6 board and maintaining the ¼" gap between boards, the width of the stand will be 17" rather than the 18". The short pieces of the support structure shown in drawing 6-5 will have to be shortened by ½" on each end. To maintain symmetry with the long non-shortened boards, maintain the 1 ¾" on the ends of the shortened pieces by making a slightly steeper angle cut. The reason I didn't choose to leave the boards at the original width was because the narrower boards look better (in my opinion) and they are less likely to warp.

- Decking boards have a "bull nose" (a slightly round) edge. Prior to cutting the 26" sections to the finished 3 3/8" width, one rounded edge was trimmed flat. The boards were then cut to the finished width. Otherwise, one side of the board would be rounded and the other flat.

- I have noticed that 4" x 4" posts are sometimes exactly 3 ½" x 3 ½", and sometimes they are slightly smaller or larger. Prior to cutting the notches in the 2" x 4" support structure to make the finger joint, the posts should be purchased and measured. The appropriate adjustments in the measurements should then be made.

- If after assembly, the square center section of the support structure is slightly larger than the upright, a wedge can be inserted into the opening and secured in place with a screw. If the center section is slightly small, the post can be trimmed with a saw, chisel, or plane.

Steel Upright

Any of the stands or benches presented thus far can be put on top of a steel upright. There are several differences when using the steel upright. These are:

- After putting this upright into the ground and securing it with either the dry mix concrete or the compacted soil method, a hole needs to be drilled into the pipe to attach the top. I place the wood top on the post and, using a combination wood/metal drill bit, drill a 5/16" hole through both the wood support and the metal pipe. Make sure the top of the wood stand is firmly seated on the top of the pipe prior to drilling any holes so that the top doesn't rock. If the wood top is firmly seated on the metal post prior to drilling the hole, only one hole needs to be drilled through the metal pipe and support to secure the top.

- Another way to secure the top is to use a 'Y' brace (drawing 6-7). Note that one brace is on the front side of the post, the other on the back side. The brace should be about one-half to two-thirds the distance from the edge of the top to the post. The 'Y' brace is secured to the post using one 1/4" bolt.

- Because the pipe is open and water can get into it, a "weep" hole needs to be drilled into the pipe at soil level to allow water to drain out. A hole 1/8" in diameter is sufficient for this purpose. When the pipe is painted during normal maintenance, you will need to check that the hole is still open and not closed with paint.

- Finally the top can also be secured to the steel post by having a steel plate welded to the post prior to setting it in the hole. A number of welding shops will weld the plate for a nominal charge. There should be holes drilled in the plate so that the top can be secured to it. The advantage of using this plate method is that no water can get into the upright, thus lessening the problem of rusting on the inside of the pipe.

Plan 5 - *Concrete Block Bench*

A rather simple bench using concrete blocks for the uprights can have some interesting effects on your display area (Picture 6-6). A schematic of this bench is presented as drawing 6-8 through 6-11.

Bill of Materials

Picture 6-6

- 2 – 8' long 2 x 4 pressure-treated boards
- 1 – 4' long 2 x 4 pressure-treated board
- 32 – 2 1/2" #8 Stainless steel screws
- 6 – concrete blocks – 16" long, 10" deep, 8" high (make sure of the size, since concrete blocks come in a number of sizes)
- 2 – concrete block tops – 16" long, 10" deep, 4" high
- 4 – pieces of ½ inch rebar 24" long (have it cut at the home improvement center)
- 2 bags dry concrete mix
- 1 bag gravel
- 1 – 8' long 2 x 4 untreated board (for form)
- 16 10p (penny) nails for form

Must-Have-Tools

- Level
- Square (either framing or carpenter)
- Saw
- Screwdriver
- Shovel

Construction

Since this type of bench is somewhat unique, it may not fit into every layout. For a rustic layout, it may be ideal. However, for the more formal exhibition layout, it may be out of place. Since it relies on the blocks for the uprights, it needs some special construction techniques.

The first thing to do is to construct the forms for the concrete pads. Each pad is about 12 inches by 18 inches finished size. Cut 4 pieces 18 inches long from the untreated two by material listed above. Then cut 4 more pieces 15 inches long. Nail one of the 15" pieces to the end of an 18" piece, and then nail the second 15" piece to the other end of the same 18" piece. Finish the form by pushing the second 18" piece between the two ends of the 15" pieces and nail them securely. The finished form should look like a rectangle and have an inside dimension of 18" by 12" (drawing 6-8). To ensure the form is square, measure the inside diagonal both ways. If the form is square, the two diagonal measurements will be the same. If one measurement is slightly longer than the other, tap the opposite diagonal until the measurements are close. For the second form repeat the same procedure with the other 4 pieces of untreated "2 by" wood.

Now lay the form on the ground where you want the bench to be, using the dimensions in the three drawings 6-9 through 6-11. Using the shovel, mark the outline of the form on the ground, remove the form and dig out the area where it is marked. Proceed with some caution since you want the finished pad to be about ½ inch under the soil line. You will, therefore, be digging out about 4 to 5 inches of soil (½ inch for the soil covering, 3 ½ inch for the pad, and 1 inch for the gravel base, if it is being used). The important thing here is that the top of the two pads must be level within themselves and with each other. The ground under the pad doesn't have to be exactly level since the gravel and concrete will compensate for any unevenness.

After the soil is dug out, pour about a 1 inch layer of the gravel into the hole. This is done to allow for moisture movement from and into the ground during the freeze/thaw cycles. Place the nailed form on top of the gravel, and level the form (See hints for the leveling operation below). Put some of the soil that was dug out around the outside of the form and gently pack the soil in so that the form doesn't move. Temporarily lay a block inside the form, allowing about an inch on each side. Drive a piece of the rebar into the ground in the center of one of the openings of the block. Then drive another piece of rebar in the center of the block opening on the other side. Continue driving each piece of rebar into the ground until they have been driven about 4 to 5 inches into the soil. Carefully remove the block, leaving the rebar standing. Repeat the process for the other form.

Using the directions on the bag of concrete mix, prepare an adequate quantity to fill both forms. Pour the wet concrete into the forms, making sure that there are no voids in the wet concrete. Using a piece of untreated "2 by" material that is about 1 to 2 inches longer than the longest side of the form, start on one side of the form and, laying the board on top of the form, move the wood piece back and forth to level the wet concrete. You will have to work the board around the two pieces of rebar. The concrete doesn't have to be as smooth as a normal sidewalk; however, the finished concrete should be relatively smooth where the concrete block will sit. Once the smoothing process is done, the concrete should be allowed to "cure" for at least 24 hours, after which time the wooden form can gently be removed from around the concrete.

Place one concrete block on each cured concrete pad about 1 inch from each edge, with the rebar sticking up in the center of each block opening. Using one of the "2 by" boards, make sure the two blocks are level with each other and each individual block is also level. If for some reason the blocks are not level, you will need to purchase a small bag of mortar mix from a home improvement center or local hardware store. Then mix up a quantity per the directions on the bag and place an amount of the wet mix under the block that is not level until it is level.

Now take some of the dry concrete mix and carefully pour it into the two openings of the block. Use a small stick or piece of wood to work the dry mix into the voids and around the rebar rod. Continue this procedure until three blocks make up the tower and the dry mix concrete has filled the inner voids and is level with the top of the last block. Make sure the three blocks form a straight vertical wall on all sides. Using a gentle spray, water the outside of the blocks and the top of the dry mix. The top of the dry mix concrete should be slightly moist; however, the blocks should be thoroughly wet. Wet one of the two solid concrete block tops thoroughly with a hose; and, when it is very damp, place it on top of the block tower. Make sure the two towers are level with each other! If they are not, you will need to mix up some more mortar to bring the solid blocks into level. Now re-wet the concrete block tower.

The top can now be built. Start with the two 8 foot pressure-treated boards and cut them in half, so that there are 4 – four foot boards. Cut the original 4 foot piece of pressure-treated board into two 17 inch pieces. Using the drawing 6-9 as a guide, draw a 90 degree line on each of the 4 four foot pieces 11 ¼" inches from each end. Now lay one of the boards on top of the block tower and make sure the lines are on the inside edge of each block tower. If the line is not on the inside edge, adjust the line on each end until both lines are on the inside edge. Once the lines are where they should be, use the square to mark the line on the sides of the board. Lay one of the 4 foot long pieces already marked on top of the two 17" pieces and adjust the board so that the pencil mark is on the outside of the 17" piece (use the drawing 6-9 as a guide). Make sure the long and short boards are square. Secure one of the 17" boards to the 4' board with one screw. Then secure the other 17" end of the board in a similar manner. Once you are sure the 17" boards are square to the 4' board, insert another screw in each piece. Continue to add the rest of the 4' pieces in the same manner, until all four 4' pieces are added. The top is then simply laid on top of the concrete blocks.

Construction Hints
- The important idea in building this type bench is that the forms are level. If one of the concrete pads is not level, the concrete blocks laid on top will not be level unless you plan on using mortar to secure the blocks. If the two pads are not level with each other, the finished height of the block verticals will not be the same and will result in the top not being level.

- When leveling the two individual forms, the following procedure can be used if the ground in between the two forms is higher than the forms. A short piece of the "2 by" material can be laid on top of each form and one of the pressure-treated 8 foot pieces can be gently laid on top of that. The level can then be laid on the 8 foot piece to get the two forms level with each other. Likewise, each individual form can be leveled using the same pieces of short boards on each side.

- When putting the removed soil around the outside of the form, the heel of your shoe can be used to compact the dirt. If the removed dirt is wet, a piece of the "2 by" material can be used to push the dirt down and around the form. The dirt doesn't need to be compacted firmly. You just need to have enough soil around the form so that it doesn't move when the concrete is added.

- When mixing the concrete, try to add only enough water to the mix to make a material with the consistency of cake batter. It is better to add less water to the mix, incorporate it all together, add a small amount of additional water and mix again, until the proper consistency is obtained. If too much water is added, it will take substantially longer for the mix to set, and the concrete will be weaker.

- Rather than pour a concrete pad for placement of the concrete blocks, prefabricated concrete stepping stones can be used. These units can be purchased from the home improvement centers in several sizes wide enough to hold the concrete blocks. The ground upon which they will be set should be leveled and compacted before putting them in place. The concrete blocks should then rest on these units. Additionally, if a concrete patio is available, the blocks could be set directly onto the patio. If either of the above alternatives is used, the blocks should not be filled with dry cement. The blocks would simply be set on top of each other. This would allow the bench to be somewhat portable.

- The concrete blocks don't necessarily need to be filled with concrete. They can be set on top of each other on the concrete base. With the wood top set on the blocks and larger bonsai on that, the block tower will be quite stable.

Plan 6 – *Long Concrete Block Bench*

This plan is a modification of Plan 5. Rather than laying the blocks in a normal fashion, the blocks are laid on their ends (Picture 6-7 and 6-8) and left unsecured, so that the benches can be moved when needed.

Bill of Materials

- 2x4 or 4x4 pressure-treated wood
- 1x6 pressure-treated decking boards
- 2" #8 Stainless screws

Must-Have-Tools

- A saw is needed to cut the decking boards and, perhaps, the support pieces
- Screwdriver
- Level
- Square

Picture 6-7 (Courtesy of Shannon Callaway)

Picture 6-8 (Courtesy Shannon Callaway)

Construction

Stack two rows of concrete blocks on the concrete pads which have been placed at the desired distance apart. Using two 2 x 4 boards (or two 4 x 4 posts if the bench is to be 8 to 10 feet) of the desired length, lay one in the front depression of the block and the other in the back depression of the block. Measure the distance between the outer edges of the two boards (allowing for some overhang if desired). Using some 1 x 6 decking boards, cut a sufficient quantity to cover the distance from end to end of the 2 x 4 (or 4 x 4) supports – allowing about ½" to ¾" between boards. Starting at one end of the support boards, make sure that the first board is at 90 degrees to the support boards. Secure it to both support boards, using two or three #8 2 inch stainless screws on each end. Then continue adding the top boards until all are in place. If the distance between the two concrete block pillars is over 8 feet and no pillar is planned for the middle, it is better to use the 4 x 4 support posts, since they will hold substantially more weight before they bend. However, it would be better to utilize a center support.

Construction Hints
- To obtain a uniform gap between boards, a scrap piece of lumber of the desired size can be laid between one secured board and the next board to be secured. Prior to attaching the loose board, a helper could gently hold the loose board in place, while you set one screw into each side. Then remove the scrap spacer board and put one or two more screws in each side.

Wood Benches

Wood top benches can be constructed in almost any length or width. Depending on the width, they can be supported with one set of center uprights (Picture 6-9), or they can have multiple legs when they are wide (Picture 6-10). They can be short – 3 or 4 foot – or they can be long – 8 or 10 feet or longer. The top boards can run parallel to the length or they can be perpendicular. The sides can be open as in Picture 6-9 or they can be closed (Picture 6-11) with a side piece. There

Picture 6-9

doesn't seem to be any constraints other than what the bonsai artist wants or can afford.

The bench pictured in Picture 6-9 consists of round uprights buried and secured with the compacted soil method. A 2x4 cross piece is attached to the supports and serves as the mount for the top boards. The top is built of three 2x6 boards spaced about an inch apart. This gives a bench about 20 inches wide.

Picture 6-10

We have chosen several designs (Plan 7, 8, and 9) that illustrate a couple of construction points and techniques. In the bill of materials, we have listed the type of building materials that can be used in the particular design, and not any specific lengths of boards. This will allow construction of any length of bench.

Plan 7 – Simple Wood Top Bench

Because I didn't like the approximate 1" gap between the top boards in the bench in Picture 6-9, I reduced the gap in this plan. I also used the square uprights. In drawing 6-12, we show a bench with a length of 6 feet and a width of approximately 18".

Bill of Materials
- 2 x 6 pressure-treated boards
- 4 x 4 pressure-treated uprights
- 2 x 4 pressure-treated boards
- #10-3" stainless steel screws
- #12-3" stainless steal screws

Must-Have-Tools
- Post hole digger
- Saw
- Screwdriver
- Level
- Wood clamps (not a must have, but will make the plumbing of the upright easier)

Construction

Construction begins with setting the uprights into the ground, temporarily plumbing them, and establishing a level line on the two end posts. However, do not secure them into the holes. Prior to cutting the uprights to height, cut two 2 x 4 boards 16 ½" long, draw a perpendicular line 6 ½" from one end, and clamp them to the uprights on the level line, with the perpendicular line on the edge of one upright . When you are sure that the two 2 x 4 cross pieces are level and there is an equal distance between both ends of the two cross pieces, firmly secure the upright into the ground using one of the previously described methods. The uprights can then be cut to the proper height. Put one #12 screw into each cross piece (leaving the clamps in place).

After the uprights are firmly in the ground, reestablish that they are perpendicular, and the cross pieces are level and at equal distances apart. Make any necessary adjustments (See Construction Hints).

Cut three 2 x 6 boards to the desired length and gently lay one of the 2 x 6 boards on top of the 2 x 4 cross pieces. Center this board so that it lies over top of the upright. I chose a length of 6 feet for the 2 x 6's. This will result in a ½ inch lip on each end. Recheck the level of the cross pieces and the 2 x 6, then drive two more #12 screws into each of the cross pieces to firmly secure them to the upright.

Now, using the #10 screws, attach the 2 x 6 to the cross piece. Place the other 2 x 6's next to the one that is secured. Maintain a ½" space between each piece and secure them with #10 screws. There should be a 1/2" overhang on each end as well as on the cross pieces.

Construction Hints
- If the uprights are secured in the ground and it is found that they are not plumb, some minor adjustments can be accomplished. For the compacted soil method of securing the uprights, take a short piece of 2 x 4, place it on the ground on the opposite side of the upright that needs to be moved slightly, and using a hammer, beat on the 2 x 4 to drive some more dirt into the hole. This often causes the upright to move slightly in the needed direction. If the dry cement method of securing the upright was used and the cement has not been in the hole for a lengthy period (more than a couple of days), a helper can push on the top of the upright, in the direction it needs to move, and the 2 x 6 center board can be attached to the cross support to hold it in place. However, if the upright is only slightly off plumb, it may be easier to accept it and proceed with attaching the top.
- Getting the two cross pieces level, the uprights perpendicular, and the distance between the two cross pieces the same, all at the same time

requires some additional hands from your helper. One way to accomplish the proper set up is to do some preliminary construction on a flat surface. After the 2 x 4 cross pieces are cut, measure a distance of 5" from one end and draw a line. Do the same for the other cross piece. Making sure your board orientation is the same lay the 2 x 4 boards on the flat surface at the required distance apart. Lay one of the 2 x 6 boards on top of the cross pieces lining up the long edge of this board with the mark on the cross pieces. The 2 x 6 should be adjusted to have a ½" overhang of the 2 x 4 both lengthwise and cross wise (see drawing 6-12). It is secured to the cross pieces with one screw. Check that the 2 x 6 is at 90 degrees to the cross piece, then drive one or two additional screws to secure it. Repeat this on the other cross piece. The other two 2 x 6 boards are then placed in position using a ½" spacer board and secured. This finished assembly can then be placed on top of the upright. The upright can then be plumbed and secured in the ground. The assembled top is removed, and the upright is cut to height. Finally, the finished assembly is placed back on the uprights and attached.

Plan 8 – *Closed Top Bench*

This design utilizes the same construction techniques used in the closed top stand (Plan 2 Drawing 6-1 and 6-2). In the drawing for this style (Drawing 6-13) we have shown a basic support structure with only two top boards installed for clarity. This design can have the outer side boards flush with the top, or with the top boards lower than the outer boards, as shown in the drawing. In drawing 6-13, the top boards are 1/2 inch lower than the side boards, which in this drawing are 1x4s.

Picture 6-11

Bill of Materials
- 2 x 4 pressure-treated boards
- 2 4 x 4 pressure-treated uprights

- 1 x 4 decking boards
- 2 x 2 pressure-treated boards
- #8-3" stainless steel screws
- #8-2" stainless steel screws
- #10-3" stainless steal screws

Must-Have-Tools
- Post hole digger
- Saw (table saw preferred)
- Screwdriver
- Level
- Square
- Clamps

Construction

The same construction techniques as in Plan 2 are used. The biggest difference is the length of the side boards, which makes it slightly more difficult to get a square corner. An easy way to do this is to secure the front board to one end of the side boards (See Sketch 6-2). These two boards can then be squared by marking equal lengths from the end of each board. Using a piece of scrap wood to hold the boards at right angles from each other, the scrap board is temporarily attached to the frame with one screw. The process is repeated with the other two boards. The two assemblies are then put together.

After the holes for the uprights have been dug, the uprights are placed in the ground and the 2 x 4's are clamped to them at the proper height. The uprights are then plumbed, and firmly set in

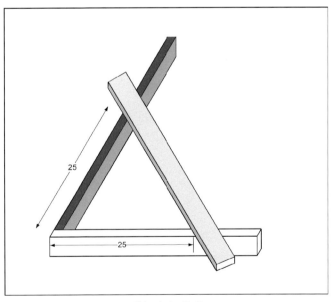

Sketch 6-2

place. The uprights are marked, the 2 x 4's are removed and the uprights are cut.

The inside support boards are cut to length and secured to the 2 uprights and the assembled 1 x 4 frame is attached to these supports. The side 2 x 2's are added to the front and back 1 x 4's of the frame at the proper distance from the top (in this case 1 ½ inch from the top). The top decking boards are then cut to length, and secured to the 2 x 2's and 2 x 4 center supports.

Construction Hints

- Using the 1 x 4, 2 x 2, and decking board, a maximum lip of 1" can be obtained. If a higher lip is desired, a 1x6 rather than the 1 x 4 can be used for the outer board. The support boards can then be adjusted in order to give a lip up to 3 inches.

Plan 9 – *Locking Support Bench*

This plan is a modification of the locking support stand previously presented as Plan 4.

Bill of Materials
- 3 - 10' long 1 x 6 pressure-treated decking boards
- 2 - 8' long 4 x 4 pressure-treated uprights
- 2 - 10' long 2 x 4 pressure-treated boards
- 1 - 10' long 2 x 2 pressure-treated boards
- #8 stainless steel screws
- #10 stainless steel screws

Must-Have-Tools
- Post hole digger
- Saw (table saw preferred)
- Screwdriver
- Level
- Wood clamps (not a must have, but will make the plumbing of the upright easier)

Picture 6-12

Construction

The first thing to decide is the length and width of the bench. For this example, I chose a length of 5' long by 21" wide. Construction is similar to Plan 4 is used (see drawings 6-4 through 6-6). The difference is the length (Drawing 6-14). I decided to use only two legs since the width is less than two feet. I also chose to use the locking finger joints and to use three underside supports, thus allowing for stability of the top while using only two uprights. I could have probably gotten away with using only two underside supports, but I didn't want to run the risk of having the top rack (i.e. twist).

This method of construction would be suitable for benches up to about 8 to 10 feet. If the bench is longer than 8 feet, I would suggest placing a third leg. For more stability, a four leg design could be used.

Construction Hints

- In making the locking finger joints, it is better to slowly 'sneak' up on the cutout width and depth. A tight joint results in a much stronger bench. Note that the shortest board has the open part of the finger joint facing down to help prevent water getting into the joint.

- If the square center section of the support structure is slightly larger than the upright, a wedge can be inserted into the opening and secured in place with a screw. If the center section is slightly small, the post can be trimmed with a saw.

- Although this design shows the wood top slats to run the length of the top, the top slats could be run perpendicular to the length since there is a support board on the ends of the perpendicular "2 by" boards. This board serves two purposes. The first is to help secure the finger joint boards from twisting or moving. The second is to have a surface to secure the outer top boards.

- One of the most important items in this design is to ensure that the two posts are level with each other and that they face each other squarely. After the holes for the supports are dug and the uprights are placed in the holes, the upright posts can be temporarily plumbed, but not secured firmly. The top can then be placed onto the two uprights and the uprights re-plumbed and either cemented in or firmed in using the compacted soil method. Once the uprights are firmly in place, they can be cut off level with each other and the top secured. Another method would be to place the uprights in the holes, clamp a long board to the uprights to make sure they face each other squarely, and then secure them in the hole.

Plan 10 – *Shohin Bench*

This bench constructed by Pauline Muth is taken from pictures printed in The Journal of The American Bonsai Society and pictures she supplied (Picture 6-13). I have slightly modified the design and do not show dimensions, allowing the reader to make the bench to fit his needs. The original dimensions are 3 feet by 5 feet. Shohin pots lose moisture faster in the hot summer sun than larger pots. The idea of this bench is to slow down this moisture loss by slightly burying the pots in haydite, turkey grit or used bonsai soil that is on the bench top. A diagram of this bench is presented in Drawings 6-15 and 6-16

Picture 6-13 (Courtesy of Pauline Muth)

Bill of Materials
- 1 x 6 pressure-treated decking boards. (Because the wood in this bench is constantly exposed to moisture, use of pressure-treated boards is highly recommended.)
- 4 - 4 x 4 pressure-treated uprights
- 2 x 4 pressure-treated boards
- 2 x 6 pressure-treated boards
- #8 stainless steel screws
- #10 stainless steel screws
- Nylon screen wire
- Haydite, turkey grit, or used bonsai soil

Must-Have-Tools
- Post hole digger
- Level

- Square (either framing or carpenter)
- Saw
- Screwdriver
- Shovel

Construction

Construction starts with loosely setting the 4 x 4 posts at the proper distances into the holes. Starting with one of the longest sides, cut a 2 x 6 to the proper length and temporarily attach one end to one of the 4 x 4 posts with a single screw. The opposite end of the 2 x 6 is leveled and temporarily attached to the second 4 x 4 post with one screw. This process is repeated on the opposite long side. The short ends are similarly secured to a 2 x 6 board. Then, starting with one upright, plumb it and either set the post in concrete or use the compacted soil method to secure it. Repeat the process with the other three uprights. Remove the 2x6 boards and cut the uprights to the desired height (about 3 to 4 feet is a good height to be able to reach into the center of the completed bench to remove the shohin bonsai). The 2x6 boards are then permanently attached to the posts so that the tops of the boards are 3.5 inches above the tops of the vertical uprights.

The inner supports are put into place – see drawing 6-15. I used 2x4 boards for the supports that run perpendicular to the long length. Although not absolutely needed, I also added 2 x 2 pieces between the 2 x 4 inner supports on the front and back 2 x 6 boards. Note that the top of the supports are also the same height as the vertical uprights. .

The decking boards are then cut to fit into the inside of the 2x6 frame, leaving about ¼" to 3/8"gap between each board (Drawing 6-16). Once cut, these boards can be secured with screws.

The screen is then placed on top of the decking board, and about 1 to 1.5 inches of the haydite, turkey grit, or used soil is placed on top of the screen. The haydite or turkey grit should be rinsed with water to remove the dust. The shohin pots are gently embedded into the grit. When watering, the shohin and haydite are all watered. This system helps keep the pots cool and they lose less water during the high heat days.

Construction Hints

- If the bench is going to be small (i.e. 2' x 4'), the post can be made from 2" x 4" pressure-treated boards. If these smaller uprights are used, it may require an additional stiffener as shown in Drawing 6-15 and Picture 6-13.

Plan 11 - *Stone Top Bench*

Stone top benches offer a completely different look and slightly different construction techniques. They won't fit into every display area but can look extremely attractive. The tops can be made of sandstone or granite. Generally, the stones are limited in size due to their weight. The additional requirement for constructing a stone top bench is to have several able bodied helpers when it is time to place the stone on the supports.

Bill of Materials
- Stone of the desired size and type
- 4x4 uprights
- ¼" Steel plates (see construction below)
- Bagged cement mix
- 3" #10 stainless screws
- Construction glue

Must-Have-Tools
- Level
- Post hole digger
- Drill and drill bits
- Stone cutting tools (potentially)

Picture 6-14

Construction

For a stone 2 foot by 4 foot, two uprights can be used. Stones larger than that will require 4 uprights. For stone tops, it is extremely important to ensure that all the upright posts are as close to level as possible. If the uprights are not level, the stone will not be level and the bonsai can slide off. When 4 posts are used and the posts are not level, the weight of the bonsai on the stone will create the possibility of the stone cracking or breaking. Additionally, stones are rarely uniform in depth, which makes placing on the uprights more problematic. To help solve this problem and to make attaching the stone to the uprights easier, a steel plate can be attached to the top of each upright with screws. Wood wedges can be slipped between the plate and stone to take care of any stone irregularities.

Picture 6-15

The steel plates can be purchased from some home improvement stores. I chose the ¼" steel plate, since that was available at my local big box store in 1 foot by 1 foot pieces along with several other sizes. That store also had ½" steel plates in the 1 square foot size; however, drilling holes in steel this thick would have been a real problem.

Because of the weight of the stone, the uprights need to have extra support in the ground. When the holes are dug for the supports, they need to be deeper than normal – about an additional 6" to 10". In addition, using a half brick in the bottom is strongly recommended. I would also suggest that the bagged cement be mixed with water prior to putting it into the post holes. Once the holes were prepared, pour some wet cement mix into the bottom of the hole, drop the brick into the hole and gently tamp it into the cement. Next the upright is placed into the hole and secured with additional wet cement. The helper constantly uses the level to ensure the post is plumb in all directions as the wet cement is added and worked around in the hole. The cement is allowed to dry for several days before additional work is undertaken.

Holes are drilled in the steel plates in order to attach them to the uprights. The holes in the plates are countersunk so that the screws will be flush with the top of the plate. The plates can then be attached to the uprights with the screws.

With aid of the helpers, the stone is placed onto the supports, centered, and the level is checked. The location of the plate is drawn onto the bottom of the stone, and the stone removed. A liberal amount of construction glue (obtained from a hardware or big box store) is applied to the plate and the stone is placed on it (Picture 6-16). The glue is allowed to dry for a day before any bonsai is placed onto the stone bench.

Construction Hints

- To make leveling the uprights easier, the full length upright is put into the hole, cement added, and then the uprights are cut to the desired height.

Picture 6-16

- Before holes are drilled in the steel plate, the center of the plate was found and the dimensions of the upright were drawn onto the plate. Three holes were drilled and counter sunk into the plate.

- One source for stone tops is kitchen cabinet stores. They have smooth granite and other types of stones which can often be purchased at a reasonable price if you are willing to take varying sizes or colors. These would be called remnants or left-overs from their intended use as cabinet tops. I would suggest staying with lighter colors, since darker colors heat up more quickly in the summer sun. Additionally, these dealers can smooth the edges of the stone. If granite is used, it will periodically need to be sealed with a granite sealer – also obtained from the cabinet top dealer. Stone obtained from these dealers have a relatively flat bottom.

- Some stone quarries can supply stone tops also. If available in your area, sandstone makes a nice looking top and can be polished to a rich sheen with auto sandpaper and mineral oil. You may have to use a carborundum saw to smooth the edges though, if the quarry doesn't do this.

Plan 12 – *Simple Shade Bench*

A shade bench, sometimes called a shade house, is nothing more than a bench with a built-in partial roof. It is designed to keep the hot afternoon sun off sensitive bonsai. As with a bench, the designs can vary from the simple to the complex. We start with a somewhat simple shade bench which can be modified to meet your need. The second design (Plan 13) is somewhat more complex, but also could be modified if so desired.

Bill of Materials
- 4 x 4 pressure-treated upright (see construction for details)
- 1 x 6 pressure-treated decking board
- 2 x 4 pressure-treated boards
- 2 x 6 pressure-treated boards
- 2" #8 stainless steel screws
- 2 ½" #8 stainless steel screws
- 3" #8 stainless steel screws
- 40 lb bag Quikrete®
- Shade cloth (see construction for details)

Must-Have-Tools
- Post hole digger
- Saw (table saw preferred)
- Screwdriver
- Level
- Wood clamps (not a must have, but will make the plumbing of the upright easier)

Construction

    Construction begins by setting 6 uprights into 6 holes (or 4 uprights in 4 holes for a shorter bench). The front uprights are 8' 4 x 4's, while the back uprights are 10 or 12' (depending on the height of the covering you prefer). The uprights are then plumbed and secured in the holes (See drawing 6-17 and 6-18) using one of the 2 x 6's to ensure the orientation of the posts, as described in previous plans. The front uprights are cut to the desired height, temporarily leaving the back ones full length. The sides and front 2 x 6's are leveled and attached with screws to the uprights. The top of the 2 x 6 boards are one inch above the front uprights. The back board is attached to the rear uprights, with the top of the board in line with the top of the two side boards. The 2x4 supports are attached inside the frame 1 inch below the top of the side boards. Although the drawing (6-17) shows two supports on each half of the structure, the actual number needed depends on the length of the bench. If the overall length of the bench is 6 feet or less, only one support on each side of the center support is needed. For every additional three to four feet of length of the bench, one additional support is required (i.e. for a bench nine to ten feet long, two supports are used on each side; for a bench twelve to fourteen feet in length, three supports are used). Don't forget to add the additional short supports to the back uprights in order to have something to screw the top to (See drawing 6-17).

The top decking boards are attached to the supports, starting with the back board. This board will have to be notched out to fit around the back uprights (See hints below). The remaining deck boards are added, leaving about a 3/8" gap between each board.

Picture 6-17

The support pieces for the top are added and the top "roof" is attached. Depending on the size bench constructed, the roof can be anywhere from ½ to 2/3 the width of the bench. Take into consideration the climate, the trees that will be placed on the bench, and how much natural shade the bench receives when you calculate the "roof". Rather than wood for the roof, the support structure can be used to hold a shade cloth (purchased from garden supply stores). These cloths come in several 'degrees' of shade, such as 30%, 50%, etc. The advantage of using these cloths is the light intensity can be changed. In early summer, a low shade number (such as 30%) can be used. In mid-summer, as the sun becomes more intense, a 50% cloth can be used.

A different type "roof" is shown in Drawing 6-19 and 6-20 and in Picture 6-17. Note that in the picture (not in the drawings) there are additional slats in the back to block some of the sun. This actual bench is exposed to the southern sun; and, to prevent tree damage, the owner had to install these slats.

Construction Hints

- If the bench is less than 6 feet, the center uprights can be eliminated.

- As with the other benches, the uprights are placed in the hole and the side panel boards are clamped to them. Once plumb, the uprights are then secured with either concrete or tamped-in soil.

- To fit the decking board around the rear uprights, the board is cut to proper length. The board is then laid into the frame, and the upright width is copied onto the deck board using a square. The depth of the upright is transferred to the board using a ruler. The three (or two) notches are cut out and the board slipped into the frame. Minor adjustments to this notch can be made with a file or a hand saw.

Plan 13 – *Large Shade House Bench*

When I was setting up my area for stands, I decided I needed a large bench to store my pre-bonsai and other small bonsai (Picture 6-18). I decided that, in addition to the bench, I would build a "covering" over the bench to block out some of the sun. This covering had to be designed to allow use of a shade cloth or some other partial sun blocker. There were two requirements to the plan. The first was that the bench had to be strong enough to hold a large amount of bonsai. The second that the plan needed to have a 'Japanese' look. After looking at a number of pictures of other bonsai enthusiasts' designs, I came up with the design in Drawing 6-21 to 6-23.

Picture 6-18

Bill of Materials
- 5 – 8' long 4x4 pressure-treated posts
- 6 – 8' long 2x6 pressure-treated boards
- 4 – 8' long 2x4 pressure-treated boards
- 4 – 10' long 2x4 pressure-treated boards
- 6 – 10' long 1 x 6 decking boards
- 3" #8 stainless screws
- 3" #10 stainless screws
- 2 ½" #8 stainless screws

Must-Have-Tools
- Post hole digger
- Electric jig saw, band saw or hand coping saw

- Saw (table saw recommended)
- Screwdriver (electric or battery-operated suggested)
- Drill
- Kreg fastening system (see Construction Hints)
- Wood clamps

Picture 6-19

Construction

Construction started with setting the 4 corner 4x4 posts. After the holes were dug and the supports placed in the holes, the posts were squared to each other and plumbed. I temporarily clamped 2x6's to the 4 posts to square them up and to get a level line at the chosen height (approximately 40" above grade). The uprights were secured using the compacted soil method, and the posts were cut to the desired height.

Two center 2 x 6 supports were added to the frame to hold the center upright posts and to help support the decking boards (see drawing 6-21 and picture 6-19). Note that there is an extra board shown in the picture that is not in the drawing. This was added because the one center board was warped and needed to be straightened.

The two 4x4 center roof supports were pre-cut to the required length prior to adding to the bench support structure. These supports were secured to the frame with 5 #10 stainless screws on each side of the frame.

The 1x6 decking boards were added to the bench to make assembly of the "roof" easier, since it could be stood on while screwing in the roof boards. The two end decking boards had to be notched, as was discussed previously.

The outer frame of the "roof" was attached to the center uprights, and two center braces were added to help hold the roof joists. The outer frame was measured prior to cutting the upper 'roof joists', to ensure the roof profiles started on the outer edge of this frame. The profiles were cut on each end of the roof joists using a jig saw and they were secured to the frame using stainless Kreg© screws.

The roof joists were set on 12" centers (Drawing 6-23). The bench was oriented so that the table top received about 50 – 75% of the midday sunlight. Therefore, it was decided to not immediately use a shade cloth or other additional sun blocking methods. However, a shade cloth can simply be laid over the roof as needed in mid-summer.

Construction Hints

- The top "roof" of this design was secured to the top frame using Kreg© screws. This is an attachment system that is used in indoor cabinetry to build cabinets without the screws showing. Stainless screws were used. The angle of the drilled hole is set by the templates with the Kreg© (See Picture 6-20 for an example). If desired, the holes can be filled in with wood plugs that match the angles drilled.

Picture 6-20

- The hardest part of this construction was the handling of the boards in the roof. A helper for this portion is highly recommended.
- The radius of the design on the ends of the roof joists is 2 ¼" for both the inside and outside curves.
- Drawing 6-22 shows two angled supports bracing the roof to the roof uprights. When the bench was built, it was decided these supports were not necessary. However, if a wider bench is constructed, they may be required.

Plan 14 – *Concrete Humidity Bench*

This definitely is a specialty bench. Its primary function is to add humidity around the bonsai sitting on the mini pedestals. It's a bench that appears to require a lot of carpentry skills, along with an extensive amount of concrete finishing skills. In addition, it is extremely heavy. Therefore the upright poles must be cemented into place in the ground. A picture of one example is shown in picture 6-21.

Picture 6-21

Bill of Materials
- 2 sheets of ¾" plywood – underlayment quality
- 3 – 8' long 2x4 boards
- Concrete reinforcing wire with 2" square opening.
- Approximately ½ yard concrete – either pre-mixed or bagged
- 4 – 8' long 4x4's pressure-treated posts.
- Construction cement
- 6p nails

Must-Have-Tools
- Post hole digger
- Level
- Saw, preferably an electric or a table saw
- Various concrete finishing tools

Construction

Construction starts with building the form (see Drawing 6-24 and 6-25). The thing to realize is that, in building the form, the finished pedestals are the depressions in the form. The outside 2x4's are cut to size and nailed together. One sheet of ¾" plywood is cut to size and the plywood is nailed to the 2x4's. To form the inner pedestals, 2x4's are cut to size and nailed in place. Note that the inner pedestals 2x4's are laid on their side.

Once the form is complete, it needs to be laid on a firm solid surface, such as a concrete driveway. The concrete reinforcing wire is cut to size, leaving about a 1 inch gap from the edge of the outside 2x4 form. When the cement is poured into the form, it will be about 2" thick over the 2 x 4's. As the cement is poured into the form, make sure it is poured slowly so that no entrained air is left; otherwise, there may be visible pockets showing in the finished product. When the wet cement has been completely added, the reinforcing wire can be pushed into the wet cement, about 1" from the top of the form. Make sure the wire is not pushed too far into the cement. It only needs to be into the cement about 1 inch.

Once all the cement has been added and the wire pushed in, take a 2x4 that is longer than the form, lay it on the 2x4's, and work it back and forth to smooth the cement level with the top of the form. Then take a cement trowel and smooth the cement.

Cover the form with a wet sheet. Periodically, spray a mist of water onto the sheet to keep it damp. Allow the cement to cure (harden) in this manner for about 4 or 5 days. Lay the second piece of plywood on the cured cement, and, with the aid of several helpers, turn the whole form over. Tap the form on all sides (including the area where the pedestal form is located) to loosen the form from the cured cement. With the aid of the helpers, raise the form off the cured cement.

Install the 4 uprights in the designated place, making sure that the tops of the uprights are all level with each other. When the top is placed onto the posts, the uprights should be about 6 to 8 inches from the edge of the completed top. Apply some construction cement to the tops of the level uprights and lay the top on them. Some of the cement may squeeze out and should be cleaned up before it hardens.

Construction Hints
- Spray the inside of the form with something like "Pam®" to make form removal easier. Some home improvement centers sell a product called 'Form Release' which also serves the same purpose.
- Once the outer 2x4's are nailed together, the cut plywood is laid on top of the 2x4 assembly and nailed to it. The inner pedestal forms have to be nailed to the plywood from the top so that the proper spacing can be maintained.
- As the concrete is poured into the form, the outer 2x4's can be gently tapped with a hammer or rubber mallet to settle the concrete uniformly into the form.

Plan 15 - *Deck Corner Stand*

Because I needed another place to put one of my bonsai, I developed this corner stand that fits over the top of the 6 inch railing on my deck. Although the space is not suitable for a lot of bonsai pots, it will hold pots less than 16 inches in width by and 10 inches in depth. Pictures 6-22 and 6-23 show the finished design and drawing 6-26 gives details of the plan.

Bill of Materials
- 2 – 8' long 2 x 2 pressure-treated board
- 2 – 8' long 1 x 6 pressure-treated deck boards

BONSAI *Your Guide to Creating* STANDS and BENCHES

- 32 – 2" #8 Stainless steel screws
- 2 – 2 ½" #8 Stainless steel screws

Must-Have-Tools

- Square (either framing or carpenter)
- Screwdriver
- Wood clamps (not a must have, but will make the assembly easier)
- Saw (preferably a table saw)

Picture 6-22

Construction

The construction of this design starts with measuring the top deck rail to get the exact width of the rail – mine was 5 9/16". Then I checked the 'squareness' of the railing – mine was fairly close.

Cut a 45 degree angle on the end of one of the 2 x 2 boards. Measure 31 inches from the point of the 45 end and make a 90 degree mark. Cut the board at the 90 degree mark. Repeat this process when cutting the remaining three boards 29 ½", 16 ½", and 15 inches. Using drawing 6-26 and picture 6-23, secure the two long pieces using one of the 2 ½" screws, making sure the orientation of the 45's are correct and the longest board is the one in which the screw is driven. Repeat the process on the shorter boards.

Picture 6-23

70

Trim off the rounded edge on one side of the 1 x 6 decking board and cut it to a finished width of 3 11/16". Cut a 45 degree angle on the end of one of the boards. Measure 44" from the point of the 45 degree angle and mark this distance. Now mark this end with a 45 degree angle at the 44" measure (see drawing 6-26 and picture 6-21). Check that the two 45 degree angles face toward each other and cut the board. Repeat the process cutting the boards 36 ¼", 28 ½", 20 ¾", and 12 ¾" at the widest point of the 45 degree angle.

Lay the long 2 x 2 assembly on a flat surface and secure the trimmed 44" decking board to it using the 2" screws. Continue securing the deck boards to the 2 x 2, leaving approximately ¼" between each board. The final piece will have to be cut to size. If the dimensions given above are used, the final piece will be 5".

Now lay the assembly over the deck rail and loosely clamp it to the deck rail. Put the short 2 x 2 assembly on the inside of the deck railing and clamp it to the main assembly, then secure the 2 x 2 using the remaining 2 " screws.

Construction Hints

- Some decks have different size railings than indicated above. If this is the case, the plan will have to be modified. The inside 2X2 assembly will either have to be lengthened or shortened to fit inside the deck rail. Otherwise it may be too long or short to match the ends of the first long deck board.

- A word of caution. The decking boards can be wider than the 3 11/16" listed above. However, the last (shortest) board needs to be at least 4" long to be able to put a couple of screws into it. If you decide to use wider boards, this last section will have to be calculated by trial and error.

- Once the 2" x 2" boards are screwed together, they can be laid on a flat surface and the top boards secured to them. If this method is used, the decking boards are temporarily fastened to the support boards using one screw in each board. This assembly should be set on top of the deck railing; and, using the railing as a guide, a pencil mark is drawn on the bottom of the top boards. The assembly can then be put back on the flat surface. However, this time the assembly is set upright with the edge of the longest board sitting on the flat surface and the balance of the assembly in the air (similar to the way it is in picture 6-23). The inside support piece can be moved into place, using the pencil mark as a guide and a screw or two used to hold it in place.

BONSAI *Your Guide to Creating* STANDS and BENCHES

Chapter 7
Finishing Up

Now that we have all the stands and benches built, we need to spruce up the area around them. When we laid out our area where the stands were to be placed (Chapter 4), we also put on the drawing a border around each individual stand or around a cluster of them. If the design chosen has individual benches placed around the area, this border may just be a simple circle to separate the grass area from the stand. You may have an area which holds a number of stands and benches. Either way, we need to finish the area so that it doesn't become overgrown with grass, weeds, or garden plants (Picture 7-1). Unfortunately, grass and weeds are tenacious and don't give up easily. There are a few things that can be done to the area that will help eliminate this problem, or at least lessen the problem.

Picture 7-1

If the area only contains grass with no garden plants, a total-kill herbicide (i.e. Roundup®) can be used to eradicate the existing weeds. This total kill herbicide will have to be used at least two or three times before all the vegetation is eliminated. Bear in mind that the chemicals in this type of product will kill the majority of plant material they come in contact with, including your bonsai. The directions on the label must be followed completely. Most of these herbicides can be purchased in ready-to-use bottles or in concentrates. In either form, they are quite expensive, as are most other garden chemicals. There are a couple of precautions that need to be highlighted:

- There should be no wind when it is time to apply these chemicals, if they are to be sprayed.

- The vegetation that is to be killed should be dry. I have found that if the vegetation is watered thoroughly the day before an application and allowed to dry overnight, the chemicals seem to be adsorbed more efficiently.
- Always remove any bonsai from the area to be treated.
- Cover any garden plants that are to be saved with plastic.
- If a sprayer is used, make sure to permanently label it with the chemical name so that it can not be used inadvertently on a bonsai.

After all the vegetation has been killed, it should be raked up, removed from the area, and the soil leveled. If the area is large, landscape fabric (sometimes called a weed block) should be laid over the selected area and pinned down. To pin the fabric down, 3" galvanized nails or clothes hangers cut into 7 to 9 inch pieces and bent into a 'U' shape can be used. Push the nails or U-shaped piece through the fabric and into fabric and into the ground to hold the fabric in place.

Picture 7-2

Some sort of mulch should then be spread on top of the landscape fabric. Rock, cypress mulch, or pine bark are a few of the coverings that have been used. A layer of about one inch should be applied for adequate coverage. Some stand areas have a combination of mulch and rock as a covering. Others have two types of rock, one as a covering and the other simulating a path.

Some bonsai artists have set their stands and benches directly in the grass area of their garden, without any cleaned up area. If this is your choice, it should be noted that the grass will grow up around the upright and have to be trimmed routinely. If cement was added to the holes where the uprights were installed and your stands will be within the grass area of the garden, the concrete should be slightly higher than the ground around it. This will stop the grass from growing

Picture 7-3

extremely close to the upright, and the grass could be kept trimmed with a lawn mower.

In a number of the pictures of stands and benches that have been presented throughout this book, most of the stands or benches have what I will call "companion plants". These plants are greenery planted around the stands. They serve several purposes: breaking up the 'starkness' of the benches or stands, adding a bit of color to the designed area complimenting the bonsai, and adding to the microclimate around the bench with a small amount of cooling. If these plants are blooming plants, they shouldn't be so eye-catching that they detract from the overall stand area. A number of plant types have been used, such as lariope, hostas, Cryptomeria, or Mugo pines, to name a few. The idea is to use small plants. Azaleas can also be used if placed judiciously around stands containing evergreen bonsai.

If there is an area of several stands placed together, as in picture 7-4, a variety of companion plants could be used. To give the 'Japanese' appearance, a small maple tree, a Hinoki cypress, or azaleas planted in the area would provide the hint of a Japanese garden.

Picture 7-4

An interesting idea was seen at one bonsai artist's garden. He used the area under the bonsai stand as a growing bed for some starts. The starts received both the water runoff and fertilizer from the stand. Beware that if starts are placed under the stand, they need to be small and shouldn't be allowed to grow long shoots that could detract from the tree on the stand.

As with the design of the stands and benches, there is no limit to what can be done at the base of the stand.

After the area has been "spruced" up and companion plants put in place, it's time to go back over each and every stand and bench to check that all screws have been driven in completely and that there are no missing screws. This is especially important where the stand is attached to the upright. For my stands, I put in 2 screws – one on the two adjacent sides. This will keep the top from rocking. I have to admit on these final inspections, I have found a top or two with only one screw.

Chapter 8

Maintenance

No matter what type of stand or bench you buy or build, some type of routine maintenance is needed. This might simply be a yearly inspection, or it might be extensive repair of wood pieces or cracked stone. It all depends on the type of weather that they are exposed to, their age, the weight of the bonsai on them, and so forth.

Water proofing

All wood structures need to be protected from the elements. If we look at a deck constructed with pressure-treated wood, it usually needs to be treated with a wood sealer every two to four years. However, if a stand is made with the same pressure-treated wood, it will probably need to be resealed every two or three years. The stand is wet every day during our normal daily watering of the trees, as well as being periodically exposed to chemical fertilizers. This causes the material used to protect the wood to degrade and exposes the wood to the elements. There is a simple way to tell if the wood needs to be resealed. Pour a small amount of water on top of the wood and see if it beads up. If it does, the wood does not need further treatment. However, if the water appears to soak into the wood, it is time – probably past time - to reseal it.

Before resealing the wood (or sealing it the first time) it should be dry and free from mildew and debris. For older stands or benches, the trees should be removed from them a couple days in advance of applying the sealer. There should be no rain for those two or three days prior to the sealer application. Before applying the sealer, check the weather forecast to make sure it isn't supposed to rain on the day the application is done. Follow the directions on the label of the sealer you purchase.

When you plan on resealing a stand, set the tree off to a distance of about five or so feet. Inspect the stand to make sure it is in good repair – if not, do whatever is needed. Then take some 220 grit sandpaper and lightly sand the top of the wood to get any of the old sealer off and to remove the "whiskers" (small filaments of wood raised by the constant watering) that have developed. Using a 50-50 solution of bleach-water and an old scrub brush, scrub the tops, underneath the top and its support pieces, and the wooden upright. Pay special attention to getting the brush down into the spaces between the boards (this also removes any mildew hiding in the crevices). Also check for any loose bonsai soil lodged in between the crevices and, remove it. The stand is hosed off with water and allowed to air dry. Prior to sealing the stand, using 220 grit sandpaper, again lightly touch up the top, and dust it off. NOTE: When sanding the pressure-treated wood, a dust mask should be worn to keep from ingesting any of the dust.

If the weather should turn to rain after you have washed the stand, it can be covered with a piece of plastic or a garbage bag, which will keep it dry until the sealer can be applied. The plastic or garbage bag should be lightly tied with a string underneath the stand's top to keep it from blowing away. Or alternately, the day for sealing can be postponed until the weather clears up and the stand can dry. The wood will never be completely dry, but the top few millimeters needs to be dry prior to applying the sealer.

While applying the sealer to the top, make sure to work the sealer down into the spaces between the boards and to the edges of the boards. Once again, follow the manufacturer's recommendation on how to apply it. Typically, this entails brushing (or spraying) on a good coat of the sealer, waiting for a short time for it to soak in, and then brushing the excess off. If possible, a time of day where the stands are not in full sunlight should be picked for the application to keep the sealer from drying out so quickly. If the stand is in sunlight all day, then early morning would be a good time for the project.

Usually the sealer will dry to the touch within a short period of time – 2 to 4 hours, depending on the temperature, wind, and how thick a coat of the sealer was applied. However, most sealer instructions I have seen recommend waiting 24 to 48 hours prior to exposing the wood to traffic. For our bonsai stands, a minimum of 24 hours is recommended to allow any organic vapors (yes, even water-based sealers have an organic constituent) to evaporate.

Inspections

All stands and benches, no matter what the design, should be thoroughly inspected at the start of the season. This should include checking that all screws or nails are tight and there are no loose boards. On stands, the inspection should include making sure the upright is not loose in the ground and that the top is level. If the top is not level, you will need to determine whether the top is loose from the upright, the upright is no longer plumb, or the wood is warped. The degree of the top being "off level" will determine what corrective action is needed. Minor tilt, less than 1 degree, will require no corrective action. For a tilt of more than 1 degree, assuming the upright is plumb, the top will need to be removed from the stand and re-secured to the upright. A small wedge laid on top of the upright may be used to level the top. However, generally, if the upright is plumb and the top is tilted, this indicates that the wooden top has warped and may need to be replaced. To determine if this is the case, a level laid from corner to corner and from the opposite corners should show if the top is the problem.

All uprights should be carefully inspected for soundness, especially at the ground level, where failure normally occurs. Take a hammer and gently tap all sides of the upright about mid-way up, listening to the sound produced. Then tap around ground level to see if there is a different sound. If the upright is rotting, a soft sound will be heard. The sound good wood releases when tapped with the hammer is what I refer to as a "solid" sound, not the "dull" sound of rotted wood.

If the sounds are different, one additional test can be performed. Using the end of the blade of a screwdriver, gently push on the area with the soft sound. If the outer wood gives way, the upright needs to be dug out and replaced. It is better to devote the time and effort to remove the upright rather than having a specimen bonsai fall to the ground when the upright collapses.

If non-stainless steel screws were used, pay particular attention to the soundness of the connections. They can rust out in one season! If you suspect that one is rusted and has given way, there are two choices to fix the problem:

- The board can be completely removed. This will probably be quite a task, since part of the broken screw may be left in one of the boards, and usually the break occurs where two boards meet.
- A new hole can be drilled close by and a new screw installed.

Stone Maintenance

There is little maintenance to be done on stone. Granite needs to be sealed every year with a sealer made especially for the purpose. Prior to sealing stone, both granite and sandstone should be inspected for cracks or 'pock' marks (small fissures caused by water seeping into a crack during the winter, freezing and causing a small portion of the top to pop out, leaving a small depression). These depressions, depending on their size, can be visually lessened by using a 400 or 600 grit sand paper with a small amount of mineral oil. A small amount of oil is placed around the outside of the fissure and the fissure is leveled out using the sandpaper. This may take some time. Periodically, the old oil should be removed and fresh oil added. Always keep the stone moist with oil as the area is sanded. An electric sander should not be used as this may take out too much of the surface.

Once the depression is smoothed out, the top should be washed with soap and water and flushed well. After it is dried, the top can be sealed.

If the depression is large, trying to smooth out the depression may not be an option. These depressions can be corrected by either adding a small amount of clear silicon caulk and smoothing it with a putty knife, or adding a small amount of epoxy cement. The epoxy should be added in several small portions to keep the epoxy within the depression.

Chapter 9
Drawings

Drawing 5-1 Square Post

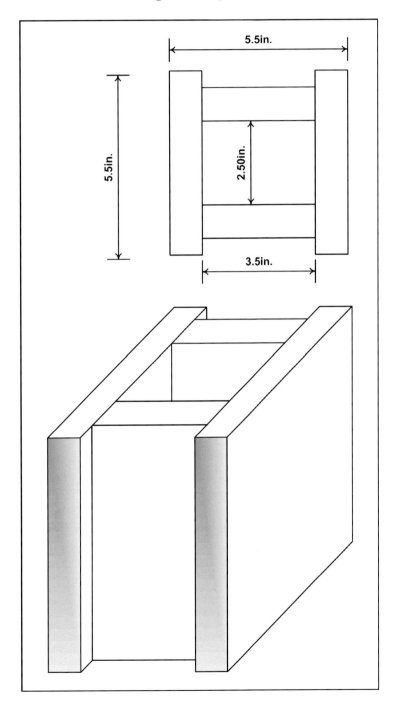

Drawing 6-1 Closed Stand Top

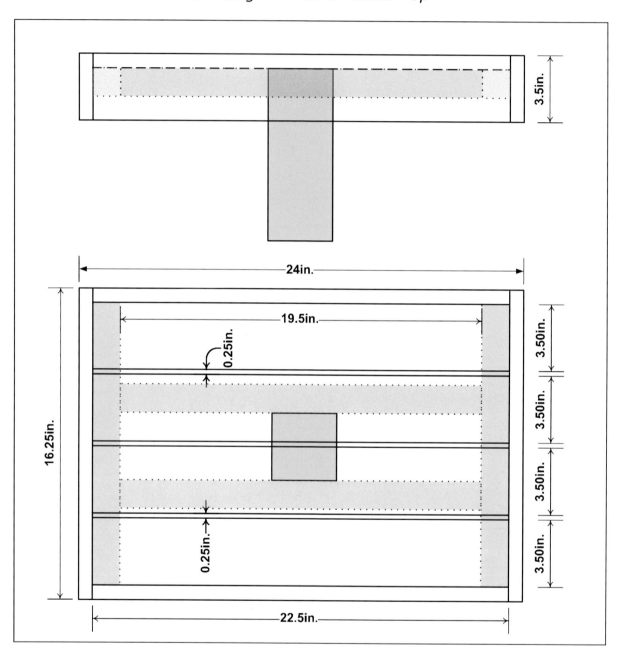

Drawing 6-2 Closed Top Stand With Lip

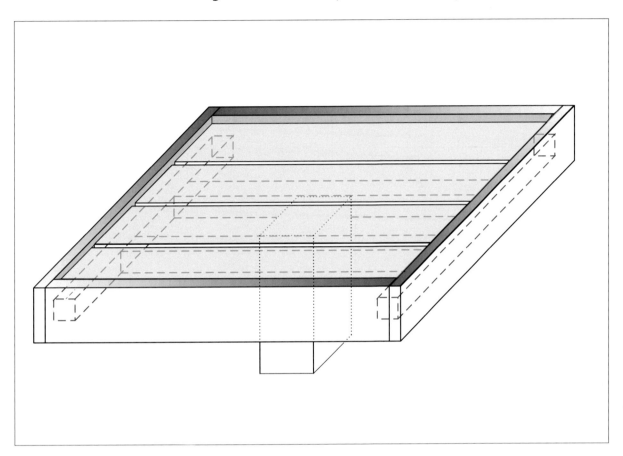

Drawing 6-3 Rotating Stand Top

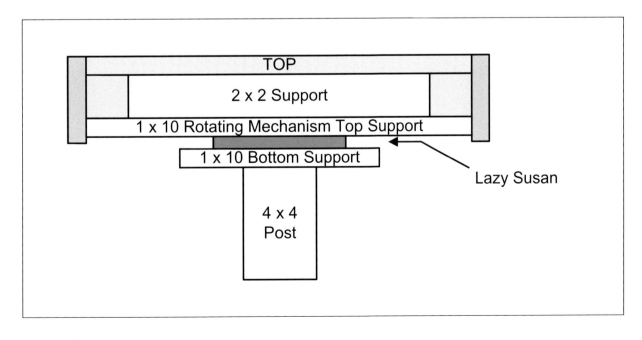

Drawing 6-4 Locking Support Wood Top Stand

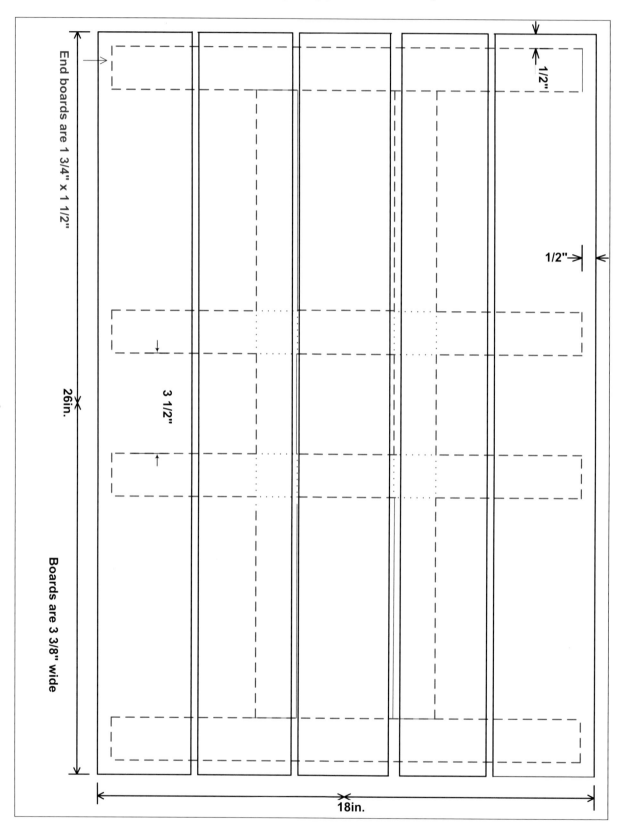

BONSAI *Your Guide to Creating* STANDS and BENCHES

Drawing 6-5 Support Structure For Locking Support Wood Stand

85

Drawing 6-6 Support Structure Assembled

Drawing 6-7 Metal Upright Support Structure

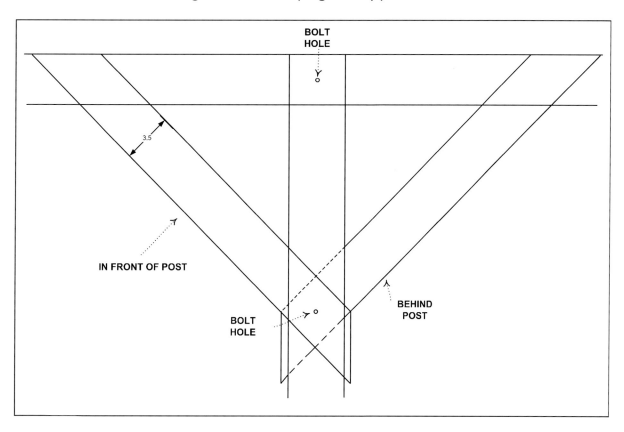

Drawing 6-8 Concrete Block Form

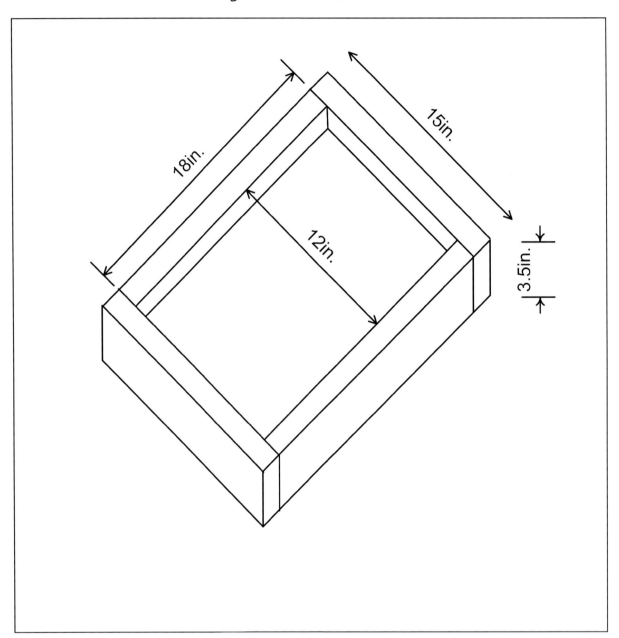

Drawing 6-9 Concrete Block Bench Top View

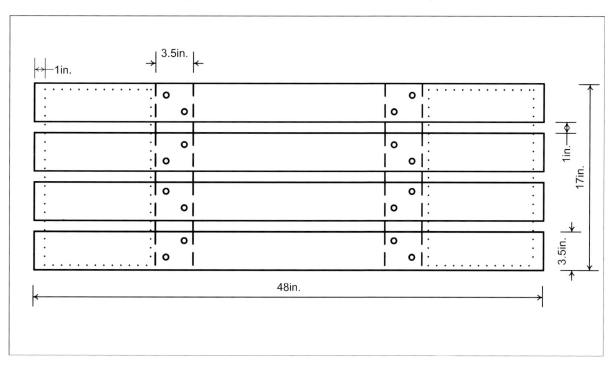

Drawing 6-10 Concrete Block Side View

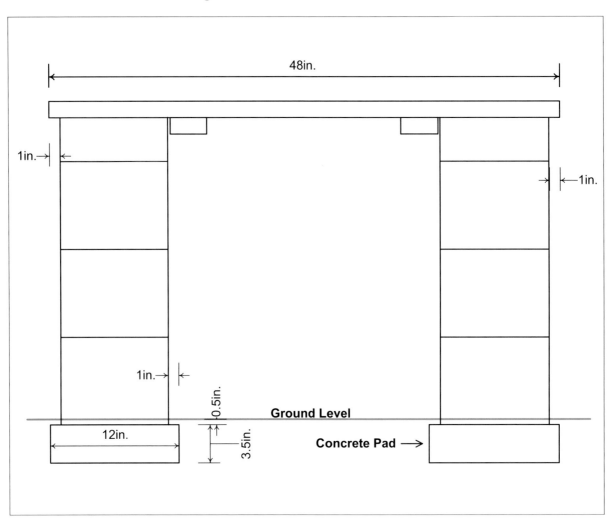

Drawing 6-11 Concrete Block Front View

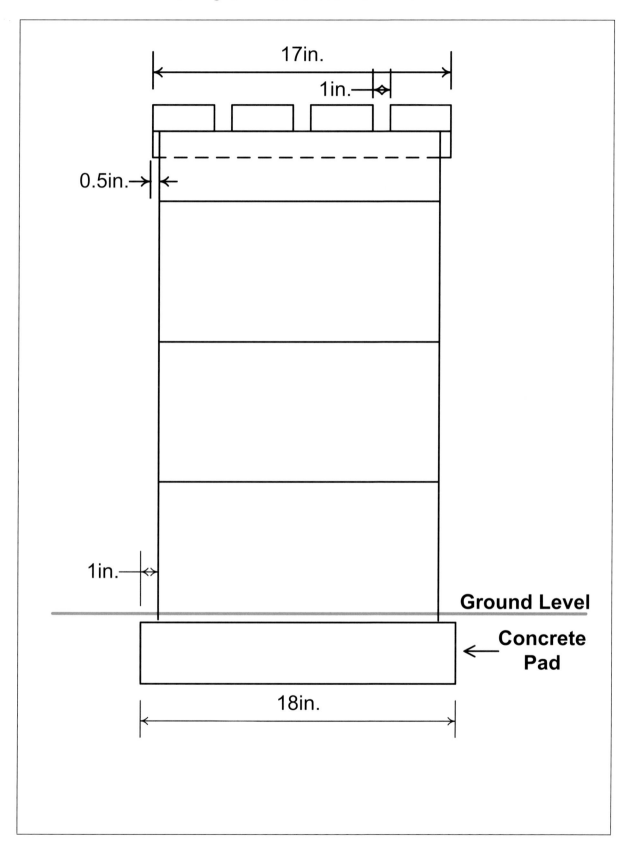

Drawing 6-12 Simple Wood Top Bench

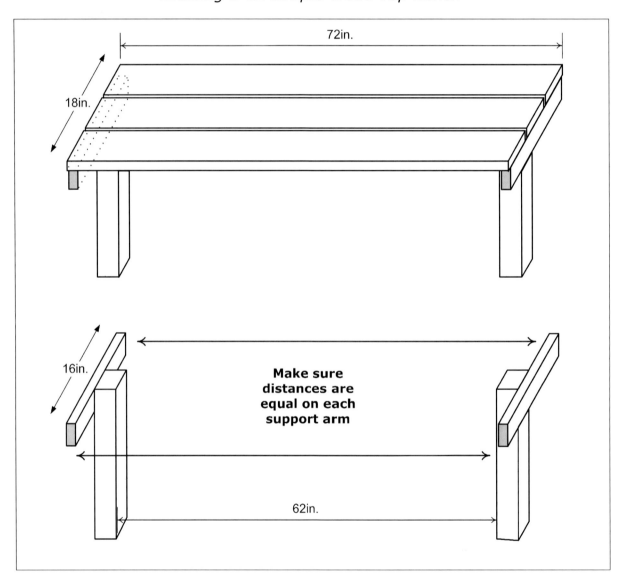

Drawing 6-13 Closed Top Bench

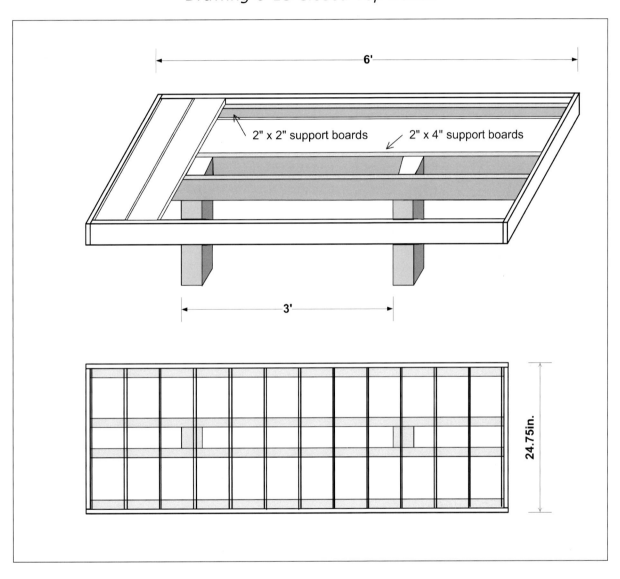

Drawing 6-14 Locking Support Wood Bench

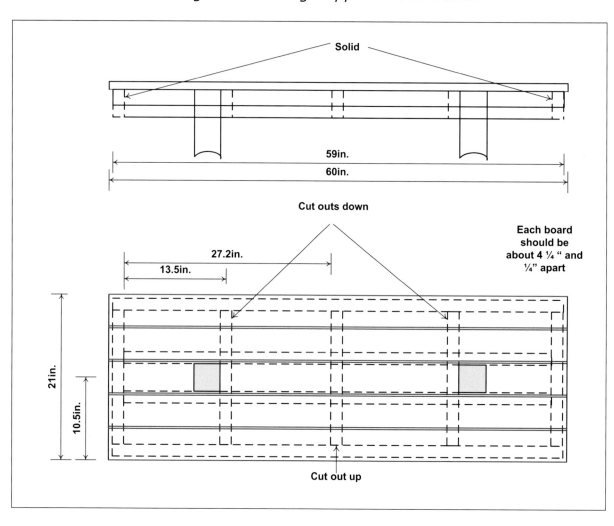

Drawing 6-15 Shohin Bench Support Structure

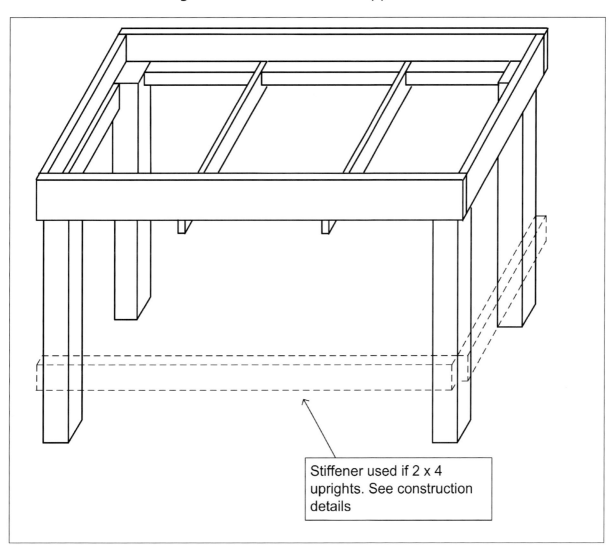

Stiffener used if 2 x 4 uprights. See construction details

Drawing 6-16 Shohin Bench

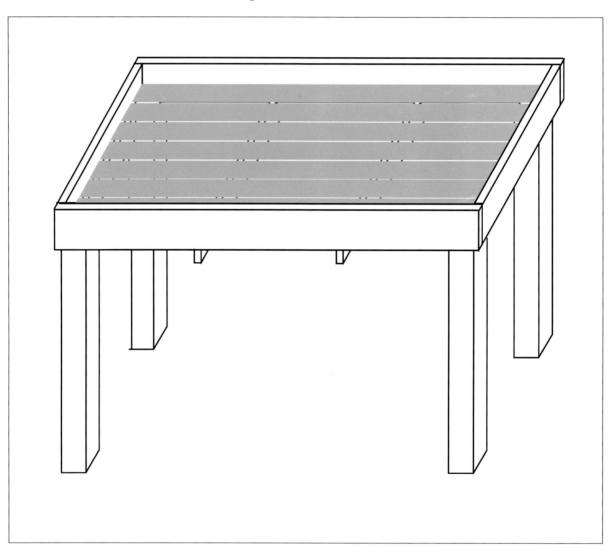

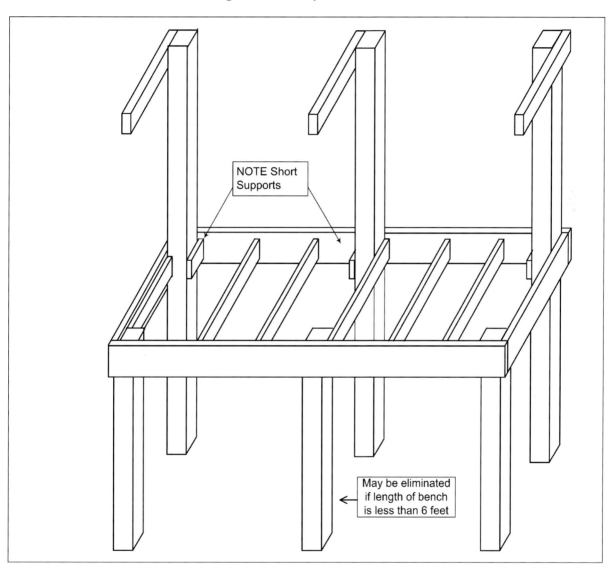

Drawing 6-17 Simple Shade Bench

Drawing 6-18 Simple Shade Bench

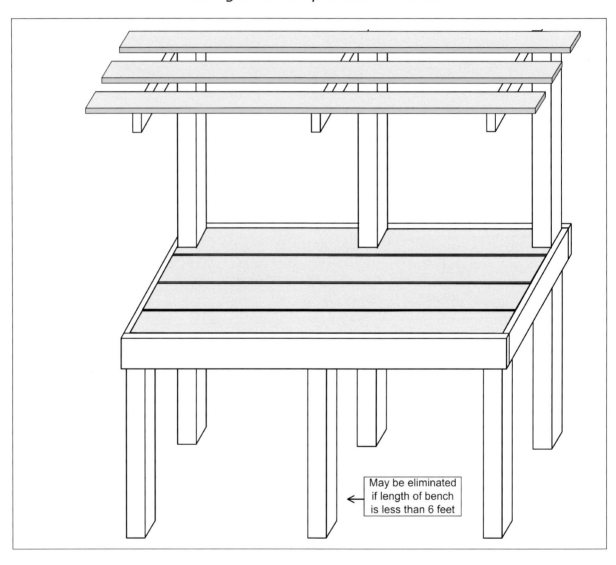

May be eliminated if length of bench is less than 6 feet

Drawing 6-19 Alternate Roof Structure To Simple Shade Bench

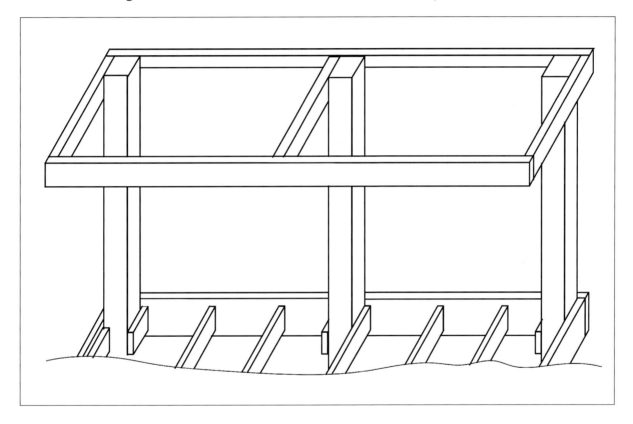

Drawing 6-20 Alternate Roof For Simple Shade

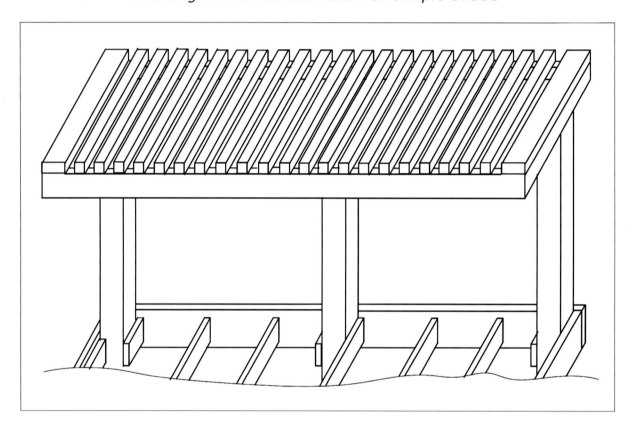

Drawing 6-21 Shade House Structure

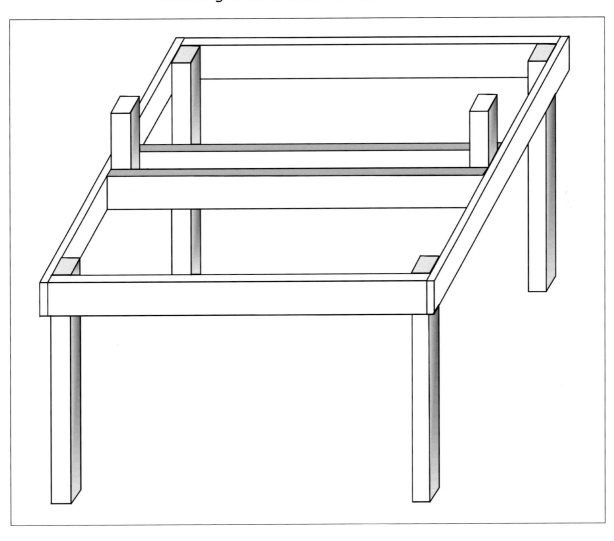

Drawing 6-22 Shade House Front Elevation

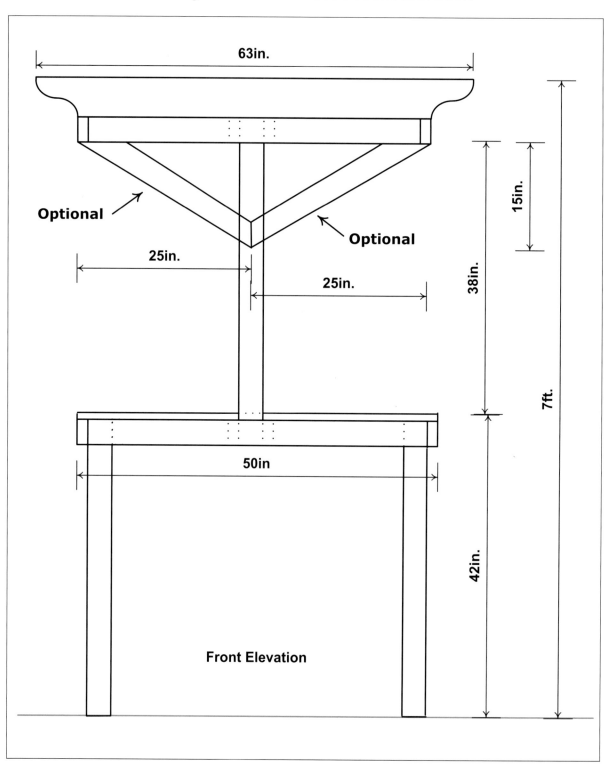

Drawing 6-23 Shade House Side Elevation

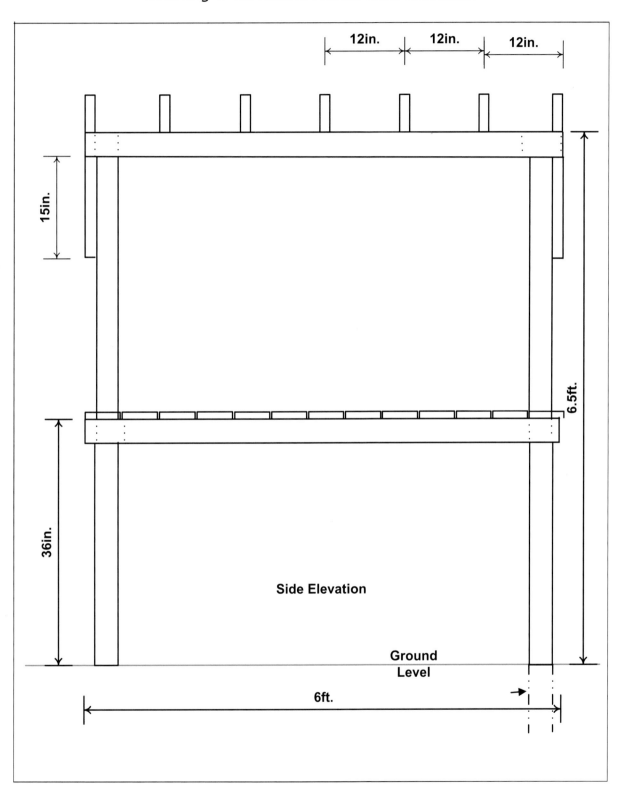

Drawing 6-24 Concrete Bench Top Form

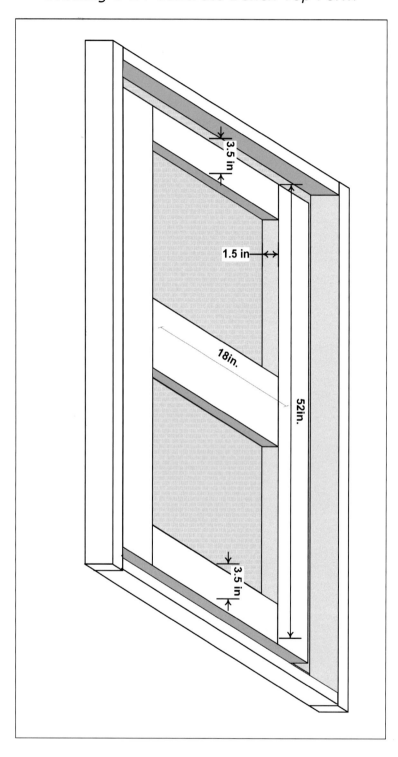

Drawing 6-25 Concrete Top Form

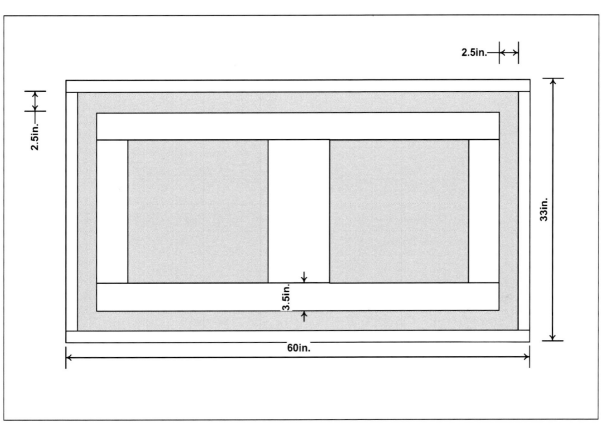

Drawing 6-26 Corner Bench

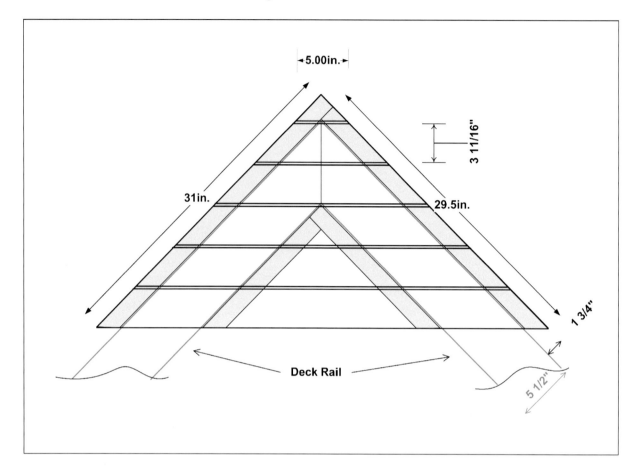

References
1. Bailey, K., *Display Benches,* Internet Bonsai Web Site,
2. Wassum, K., *Recipe For A Bonsai Bench,* Puget Sound Bonsai Association Web Site
3. Ruckman, F, *Bonsai Bench,* Bonsai By Design, Newsletter of the Greater Evansville Bonsai Society, Oct, 2004
4. Muth, P. Journal of The American Bonsai Society, Vol. 40, No. 4, page 5 and Vol. 41, No. 1, page 9.

INDEX

B

Bench Tops 27

C

Concrete blocks............................26
Concrete pads 47
Construction Glue 31
Cupping..34

D

Drawing 5-1 Square Post 81
Drawing 6-1 Closed Stand Top 82
Drawing 6-2 Closed Top Stand With Lip..................................83
Drawing 6-3 Rotating Stand Top 83
Drawing 6-4 Locking Support Wood Top Stand..............................84
Drawing 6-5 Support Structure For Locking Support Wood Stand 85
Drawing 6-6 Support Structure Assembled............................86
Drawing 6-7 Metal Upright Support Structure.............................87
Drawing 6-8 Concrete Block Form....88
Drawing 6-9 Concrete Block Bench Top View..............................89
Drawing 6-10 Concrete Block Side View....................................90
Drawing 6-11 Concrete Block Front View....................................91
Drawing 6-12 Wood Top Bench 92
Drawing 6-13 Closed Top Bench........93
Drawing 6-14 Locking Support Wood Bench 94
Drawing 6-15 Shohin Bench Support Structure.............................95
Drawing 6-16 Shohin Bench.............96
Drawing 6-17 Simple Shade Bench Structure.............................97
Drawing 6-18 Simple Shade Bench ..98
Drawing 6-19 Alternate Roof Structure To Simple Shade Bench 99
Drawing 6-20 Alternate Roof For Simple Shade Bench 100
Drawing 6-21 Shade House............101
Drawing 6-22 Shade House Front Elevation..............................102
Drawing 6-23 Shade House Side Elevation 103
Drawing 6-24 Concrete Bench Top Form....................................104
Drawing 6-25 Concrete Top Form...105
Drawing 6-26 Corner Bench 106
Dry Mix Concrete.........................30

F

Flue tile 27

H

Helpers..36

I

Inspections 78

K

KDAT wood..................................33
Kreg© screws...............................67

L

Landscape timber.........................25
Laser level...................................35

P

Plan 1 - Wood Stand........................37
Plan 2 - Closed-Top Wood Stand 39
Plan 3 - Rotating Closed-Top Wood Stand...................................41
Plan 4 - Locking Support 43
Plan 5 - Concrete Block Bench........46
Plan 6 - Long Concrete Block Bench 50
Plan 7 - Simple Wood Top Bench..... 52
Plan 8 - Closed Top Bench 54
Plan 9 - Locking Support Bench.......56
Plan 10 - Shohin Bench 58
Plan 11 - Stone Top Bench 60
Plan 12 - Simple Shade Bench..........62
Plan 13 - Large Shade House Bench .65
Plan 14 - Concrete Humidity Bench ..67
Plan 15 - Deck Corner Stand 69
Plumb..37
Post hole digger 35

S

Sandstone **28**
Saw **35**
Shovel **35**
Stainless screws **29**
Stand Tops **27**
Steel Upright **45**

T

Tools **34**

U

Uprights **25**

W

Water proofing **77**
Wood Benches **51**
Wood level **35**
Wood Sealer **30**